What About Tongue - Speaking?

What About
Tongue-Speaking?

by

ANTHONY A. HOEKEMA

Professor of Systematic Theology
Calvin Theological Seminary
Grand Rapids, Michigan

WILLIAM B. EERDMANS PUBLISHING COMPANY
GRAND RAPIDS, MICHIGAN

First printing, March 1966
Second printing, September 1973
Third printing, May 1976

Printed in the United States of America.
Library of Congress Catalog Card Number: 65-28568

ISBN 0-8028-1557-X

Preface

My main purpose in this book is to make a Biblical and theological evaluation of the phenomenon of tongue-speaking. A brief historical survey of glossolalia is included, as is also a chapter asking what the church at large can learn from the tongue-speaking movement.

I should like to make clear at the outset that I am very grateful for what God is accomplishing through Christians of Pentecostal persuasion, particularly on the mission fields of the world. I look upon Pentecostals and Neo-Pentecostals as brothers in Christ, and therefore what I shall be saying about their views on the tongues question I shall be saying in a spirit of Christian love. I should like to have my Pentecostal friends consider this book a kind of theological conversation with them, with the purpose of arriving at a better understanding of what God's Word teaches about the subject under discussion.

I have based my exposition of the teachings of Pentecostals and Neo-Pentecostals primarily on their own writings, leaning particularly on two doctrinal books by Assembly of God writers: Carl Brumback, *What Meaneth This?* and Ralph M. Riggs, *The Spirit Himself*. I have tried to be fair and accurate, but there are bound to be inadequacies. I shall be grateful if any inaccuracies are called to my attention.

This book grew out of a series of lectures given in October, 1964, at the Conservative Baptist Seminary in Denver, Colorado. For the invitation to deliver these lectures, and for the warm hospitality shown me there, I remain deeply grateful.

I wish to express my appreciation to all who sent material, provided information, and answered correspondence. I am indebted to various authors who have written on glossolalia, and to various individuals with whom the subject was discussed. I should like also to thank my students at Calvin Seminary, whose questions aroused my interest in this subject.

I am grateful above all to the Lord who enabled me to make this study. May this book magnify the Father who chose us, the Son who died for us, and the Holy Spirit who dwells within.

ANTHONY A. HOEKEMA

Grand Rapids, Michigan

Contents

Preface   5

Abbreviations   8

1. THE HISTORY OF TONGUE-SPEAKING   9

2. THE SIGNIFICANCE OF TONGUE-SPEAKING FOR
   PENTECOSTALS   35

3. A BIBLICAL EVALUATION OF TONGUE-SPEAKING   49

4. A THEOLOGICAL EVALUATION OF TONGUE-SPEAKING   103

5. WHAT WE CAN LEARN FROM THE TONGUE-SPEAKING
   MOVEMENT   125

Bibliography   151

Index of Subjects   157

Index of Scriptures   161

ABBREVIATIONS

KJ   King James Version
ASV American Standard Version

Note: All Scripture quotations not otherwise identified are from the King James Version.

Facts of publication for most books mentioned in the footnotes will be found in the bibliography; for books not listed in the bibliography, these facts will be in the footnotes.

1

The History of Tongue-Speaking

THE LAST FEW YEARS HAVE WITNESSED A REMARKABLE revival of interest in a phenomenon commonly known as "tongue-speaking." The name itself tells us very little; obviously all speaking is done with the tongue. What is so unusual about "speaking in tongues"?

Tongue-speaking, or *glossolalia,* to use the technical term, is a spontaneous utterance of sounds in a language the speaker has never learned and does not even understand. This tongue-speaking is usually done only in certain types of religious groups.

What is surprising, however, is that, though for a long time tongue-speaking was largely confined to Pentecostal churches, for the past five years this phenomenon has been spreading to the major denominations of Christendom. Tongue-speaking has broken out among high-church Episcopalians, Presbyterians, Methodists, Baptists, Lutherans, and Reformed. As glossolalia spilled over from store-front churches and Pentecostal tabernacles to Gothic sanctuaries and suburban living rooms, news wires began to hum, typewriters clicked, and presses whirled. Almost overnight, speaking in tongues became front-page news.

Although tongue-speaking on a large scale did not begin until the rise of Pentecostalism in 1906, the phenomenon did appear previous to that date, both within and without the Christian church. Within the church, however, until the beginning of the twentieth century, tongue-speaking was encountered only occasionally, among minority groups.

To understand the current manifestation of glossolalia,[1] we must know something of its history. In giving this brief history I do not plan to discuss tongue-speaking outside the Christian church, though one can find many interesting parallels to this phenomenon among devotees of non-Christian religions.[2] Neither do I plan to discuss at this time the Biblical references to glossolalia, since these will be treated in subsequent chapters. I should like to begin this brief historical survey at about A.D. 100, since this date marks the approximate end of what we might call Biblical history and the approximate beginning of what we usually call church history. The historical treatment will be divided into three phases: from A.D. 100 to A.D. 1900, the Pentecostal movement, and Neo-Pentecostalism.

From A.D. 100 to 1900

As we survey this history of the Christian church, what strikes us is the relative infrequency of glossolalia. What also strikes us is that the groups among whom tongue-

[1] This word, derived from the Greek words *glōssa*, tongue, and *lalia*, speaking, will be used as a synonym for tongue-speaking.

[2] Cf. J. Behm, γλῶσσα, in *Theological Dictionary of the New Testament*, ed. Gerhard Kittle, trans. Geoffrey W. Bromiley (Grand Rapids: Eerdmans, 1964), I, 722-24. See also E. Mosiman, *Das Zungenreden geschichtlich und psychologisch untersucht*, pp. 39-43.

speaking occurred were minority groups, often under persecution. The question we must face, as we examine this history, is this: are we compelled to assume that these occurrences of glossolalia were continuations of the charismatic gift of tongues as it occurred, say, at Corinth; or is it possible that there may be psychological explanations for this phenomenon which make the former assumption unnecessary and even erroneous?

1. *Montanism.*

Pentecostal writers sometimes refer to Montanism as a movement in the ancient church of the second century A.D. which is akin to their own. One of these writers puts it this way: "A sect in the ancient Church that can be classed as Pentecostal was that founded by Montanus of Phrygia, who advocated strict church discipline and believed that the Church was to receive a new Pentecostal baptism."[3] The same author quotes Eusebius, the fourth-century church historian, to the effect that Montanus "was carried away in spirit, and wrought up into a certain kind of frenzy and irregular ecstasy, raving, and speaking, and uttering strange things."[4] Montanus' two female companions, Prisca and Maximilla, are also said to have spoken "in a kind of ecstatic frenzy."[5]

If, however, Montanism be cited as a precedent for Pentecostalism, it is a rather unhappy precedent, since the church judged Montanus' teachings to be heretical. His position was that the age of the Spirit had come, and that the Spirit now spoke through Montanus. New revelations were received by him, supplementing and augment-

---

3 Klaude Kendrick, *The Promise Fulfilled,* p. 18.

4 *Ibid.,* p. 19. The reference in Eusebius is to the *Ecclesiastical History,* trans. C. F. Cruse (London: Bell and Daldy, 1870) , p. 184. This is in Book V, Chap. 16.

5 Eusebius, *op. cit.,* Book V, Chap. 16.

ing the Bible. Since the final age had now been ushered in, Montanus and his associates urged people to assemble at Pepuza, in Phrygia, to await the end of the world. Montanus and his followers were excluded from the church because the claim to have received revelations superior to the Bible was judged to be contrary to the finality of Scripture. Though it cannot be denied, therefore, that tongue-speaking occurred among the Montanists, the fact that it occurred among the members of this group hardly constitutes a strong recommendation.

2. *The Testimony of Irenaeus* (ca. A.D. 130-200).

The passage most commonly quoted from Irenaeus as indicating the continuation of glossolalia in the ancient church is found in his *Against Heresies*, V, 6, 1:

> For this reason does the apostle declare, "We speak wisdom among them that are perfect," terming those persons "perfect" who have received the Spirit of God, and who through the Spirit of God do speak in all languages, as he used himself[6] also to speak. In like manner we do also hear many brethren in the Church, who possess prophetic gifts, and who through the Spirit speak all kinds of languages, and bring to light for the general benefit the hidden things of men, and declare the mysteries of God, whom also the apostle terms "spiritual," they being spiritual because they partake of the Spirit, and not because their flesh has been stripped off and taken away, and because they have become purely spiritual.[7]

This passage is frequently quoted by Pentecostals to prove that in the second century A.D. there were people who spoke in "all kinds of languages." Both P. Feine and G. B. Cutten, however, point out that, since the word

---

[6] Though the translation here has Himself, this is obviously an error, since the reference is to Paul and not to the Spirit.

[7] *The Ante-Nicene Fathers*, eds. Alexander Roberts and James Donaldson (Grand Rapids: Eerdmans, 1956), I, 531.

translated "all kinds of" is a somewhat obscure term (the Greek here, supplied by Eusebius of Caesarea, has *pantodapais*), it is not certain whether Irenaeus is speaking of foreign languages or of ecstatic utterances which were not in specific known languages.[8]

Let us look at this passage a bit more carefully, however. The following comments about it are in order: (1) When Irenaeus describes, in II, 32, 4, the miraculous gifts of the Spirit still in the church in his day, he mentions exorcism, foretelling the future, visions, prophecy, healing, and even raising the dead (though B. B. Warfield argues that this last reference refers only to people who had been raised from the dead in apostolic times and of whom Irenaeus has heard).[9] In this listing of the the gifts of the Spirit, however, Irenaeus does not mention speaking with tongues. Why not? If the gift were still in existence in his day one would expect him to mention it here alongside of prophecy and healing.

(2) In V, 6, 1, the passage quoted above, Irenaeus' main point is not to discuss gifts which may still be present in the church, but to explain that the terms *perfect* and *spiritual,* when used by the Apostle Paul, do not in any way devaluate man's body. The general argument of this section concerns the doctrine of the resurrection of the body, which the Gnostics denied. What Irenaeus here says about people who "through the Spirit speak all kinds of languages," therefore, is purely incidental to his purpose. In other words, the point he is making here would be made equally well whether he were talking about

8 P. Feine, "Speaking with Tongues," *Schaff-Herzog Encyclopedia of Religious Knowledge* (Grand Rapids: Baker, 1960), XI, 37; George Barton Cutten, *Speaking with Tongues,* p. 33.

9 Benjamin B. Warfield, *Miracles Yesterday and Today,* pp. 13-16.

people in New Testament times or about people of his own day.

(3) There is some possibility that Irenaeus is here speaking, not about a phenomenon which was occurring in his day, but about what had happened in New Testament times. This is certainly true of the first sentence of the quotation, where the editor has inserted a footnote referring the reader to I Corinthians 2:6; Irenaeus is here speaking of people in the Corinthian church who through the Spirit of God spoke "in all languages." The second sentence, describing brethren in the church who not only speak with tongues but also have prophetic gifts, bring to light hidden things, and declare the mysteries of God, ends with the statement: "whom also the apostle terms 'spiritual.' "[10] The word translated "terms" is *vocat* in the Latin, a present indicative form of the verb *vocare*, "to call or name." These people, Irenaeus is saying, Paul calls "spiritual." If Irenaeus meant to say that certain people in his own day were the kind of people whom Paul would have called spiritual if he were now living, why was this not made more clear? Why did Irenaeus not use a perfect subjunctive instead of a present indicative? It is also significant that the spiritual gifts spoken of in this second sentence are precisely the ones described in the First Epistle to the Corinthians, to which the first sentence of the quotation alludes. It is therefore possible that Irenaeus is not speaking here about a phenomenon occurring in his day, but simply about what had happened in New Testament times.

---

[10] Unfortunately, we do not have the Greek text at this point. The Latin text, however, reads: "quos et spirituales Apostolus vocat" (Migne, *Patrologia Graeca*, VII, 1137). Note that the *et* precedes the word *spirituales*. The point is: here is a different term which the Apostle uses for a similar group of people. Hence a better translation would be: "whom the Apostle also terms 'spiritual.' "

(4) It must be admitted, however, that Eusebius, the church historian, did understand Irenaeus to be describing something that was occurring in the second century A.D.[11] And the opening words of the quotation do seem to give the reader that impression: "In like manner we do also hear[12] many brethren in the Church . . . who through the Spirit speak all kinds of languages. . . ." The words "in like manner" and the repetition of "tongue-speaking" (which had already been mentioned in the preceding sentence) would make one think that Irenaeus is referring to something going on in his own day. If so, we do have evidence for the continuation of the gift of tongues into the second century, though we are not told whether these tongue-speakers were Montanists or members of the regular churches. And there remains the puzzle about the meaning of the words, "whom the Apostle also terms 'spiritual.' "

3. *Tertullian* (*ca.* 160-220).

There is a passage in Tertullian in which he indicates that an ecstatic type of speech was common in his own group. In his book *Against Marcion* he challenges Marcion to show him phenomena such as the following:

> Let Marcion then exhibit, as gifts of his god, some prophets, such as have not spoken by human sense, but with the Spirit of God, such as have both predicted things to come, and have made manifest the secrets of the heart; let him produce a psalm, a vision, a prayer — only let it be by the Spirit, in an ecstasy, that is, in a rapture [*amentia*], whenever an interpretation of tongues has occurred to him; let

11 *Ecclesiastical History*, V, Chap. 7.

12 It should be noted, however, that in the Latin text the verb *to hear* is in the perfect tense: *audivimus*, that is, *we have heard*. In this connection Warfield's comment is significant: "Irenaeus' youth was spent in the company of pupils of the Apostles. . ." (*op. cit.,* p. 25). Irenaeus may simply be reporting here what he had heard, as a young man from those who had been with the apostles.

him show to me also, that any woman of boastful tongue in his community has ever prophesied from among those specially holy sisters of his. Now all these signs (of spiritual gifts) are forthcoming from my side without any difficulty. . . .[13]

Two things are to be noted about this quotation, however: (1) Tertullian was a Montanist when he wrote *Against Marcion.* We have already seen that the fact that glossolalia occurred among the Montanists can hardly be construed as an endorsement of it. (2) In the entire passage nothing is said about glossolalia, though something is said about an interpretation of tongues. Speaking in ecstasy is mentioned, speaking in a rapture *(amentia,* suggesting that the conscious mind was not in control), but it is not specifically stated that this included speaking in an unknown tongue. One could speak in ecstasy in a known language.

4. *Chrysostom (ca.* 345-407).

Chrysostom, a fourth-century father, gives clear testimony that there was no glossolalia in the church in his day. In commenting on Paul's discussion of tongue-speaking in I Corinthians 12 and 14, he says, "This whole place is very obscure; but the obscurity is produced by our ignorance of the facts referred to and by their cessation, being such as then used to occur but now no longer take place."[14]

5. *Augustine* (354-430).

Augustine also testified that he observed no glossolalia in the church of his day. For in his sixth homily on I John he wrote:

---

[13] V, 8, quoted from *Ante-Nicene Fathers,* III, 446-47.
[14] *Homilies on the First Epistle of Paul to the Corinthians,* XXIX, 1, in *Nicene and Post-Nicene Fathers, First Series,* Vol. 12.

In the earliest times, "the Holy Ghost fell upon them that believed: and they spake with tongues," which they had not learned, "as the Spirit gave them utterance." These were signs adapted to the time. For there behooved to be that betokening of the Holy Spirit in all tongues, to shew that the Gospel of God was to run through all tongues over the whole earth. That thing was done for a betokening, and it passed away. In the laying on of hands now, that persons may receive the Holy Ghost, do we look that they should speak with tongues? Or when we laid the hand on these infants [editor's note: the neophytes, or new converts], did each one of you look to see whether they would speak with tongues, and, when he saw that they did not speak with tongues, was any of you so wrong-minded as to say, These have not received the Holy Ghost; for, had they received, they would speak with tongues as was the case in those times?[15]

He also asserted, in another writing, "For who expects in these days that those on whom hands are laid that they may receive the Holy Spirit should forthwith begin to speak with tongues?"[16]

It would seem, therefore, that by the time of Chrysostom there is no evidence of glossolalia in the Eastern church, and that by the time of Augustine there is no trace of tongue-speaking in the Western church.[17] A question we

[15] *Homilies on the First Epistle of John*, VI, 10, in *Ibid.*, Vol. 7.
[16] *On Baptism, Against the Donatists*, III, 18, 16.21 in *Ibid.*, Vol. 4.
[17] A prominent Pentecostal writer quotes Augustine as saying, "We still do what the apostles did when they laid hands on the Samaritans and called down the Holy Spirit on them by the laying on of hands. It is expected that converts should speak with new tongues" (Carl Brumback, *What Meaneth This?*, p. 91). The same quotation is found in Stanley H. Frodsham, *With Signs Following* (1946 ed.), p. 254; and in John L. Sherrill, *They Speak With Other Tongues*, p. 83. In no case, however, is any documentation given for this statement. In view of the documented quotations given above, which convey quite the opposite impression, can we be certain that Augustine really said what Brumback and Frodsham claim that he said?

are moved to ask already at this point is this: if glossolalia is as important a gift of the Spirit as present-day Pentecostals and Neo-Pentecostals say it is, why did God allow it simply to disappear from the church? We have found glossolalia among the Montanists, but there it was associated with a sectarian movement which denied the finality of Scripture. The statement in Irenaeus which is cited by many may, as we have seen, be a description of tongue-speaking in New Testament times rather than of a phenomenon occurring in Irenaeus' own day.

6. *The Middle Ages.*

George Barton Cutten's *Speaking with Tongues* is hailed by students of the subject as the most thorough older history of tongue-speaking in the English language. His comment about the relative absence of glossolalia during the Middle Ages is quite interesting: "It is rather surprising . . . that in this age of wonders [the medieval period] it [the gift of tongues] appeared so infrequently" (p. 37).

A number of individuals in the medieval period are said to have spoken with tongues, particularly in foreign languages which they never learned. St. Vincent Ferrier (1357-1419) is said to have been understood by Greeks, Germans, and Hungarians, though he spoke to them in the dialect of his native Valencia.[18] St. Louis Bertrand (1526-81) is supposed to have converted 30,000 South American Indians of various tribes and dialects through the use of the gift of tongues.[19] It is also reported that St. Francis Xavier (1506-52) had so remarkable a gift of tongues that he was able to preach to natives of India, China, and Japan in their own languages, though he had

[18] Cutten, *op. cit.*, p. 42.
[19] *Ibid.*, pp. 46-47.

never learned them.[20] Cutten goes on to point out, however, that these reports contradict both the testimony of Xavier himself and the explicit declarations of historian Joseph Acosta. The latter states that Xavier had to work very hard to master the Japanese language and other languages which he studied.[21] And the *Encyclopedia Britannica* article on Xavier specifically mentions the fact that he favored the study of native languages by missionaries.[22] When we see how the process of embellishing the history of saints with fantastic legends was operative in the case of Xavier, we learn to take with more than a grain of salt other medieval claims for the miraculous gift of foreign tongues.

At the time of the Reformation some of the best minds of Europe searched the Scriptures diligently to rediscover the New Testament patterns of doctrine and life. Not one of the Reformers, however, found that tongue-speaking belonged to the normal gifts God had permanently bestowed on the church.

7. The Little Prophets of the Cevennes.

As we move along into the modern period, we should briefly note what is said about the glossolalia of the so-called "Little Prophets of the Cevennes." After the Revocation of the Edict of Nantes in 1685, many Protestants left France, and life became increasingly difficult for those who remained. From 1685 to the early 1700's the poor Huguenot peasants of the Cevennes region of Southern France had to suffer unmentionable outrages and cruel persecutions. During the persecutions many of these

20 *Ibid.,* pp. 42-45.
21 *Ibid.,* p. 46.
22 1964 ed., XXIII, 836.

peasants became prophets; it is especially interesting to note that a great number of these prophets were children. These prophets of the Cevennes used to fall into ecstasies and to utter words which they believed to have been inspired by the Holy Spirit. Some of them were said to have spoken in Hebrew and Latin, though they had never learned these languages. One of them said that the spirit of an angel or of God Himself made use of his organs of speech; he was certain that a higher Power spoke through him.[23]

Other interesting things are told about these Camisards, as they have also been called: lights in the sky are said to have guided them to places of safety, and voices are said to have sung encouragement to them. Warfield notes that, in common with the ancient Montanists, they predicted the speedy coming of the Lord and the setting up of His personal reign on earth, claiming that the diffusion of spiritual gifts evident in their movement was a preparation for and a sign of this imminent return. Warfield also tells about their prediction that a certain Dr. Emes, who had died on December 22, 1707, would rise again on March 25, 1708. Unfortunately, Dr. Emes did not do so, and hence the prophets had to publish a pamphlet giving "Squire Lacy's reasons why Dr. Emes was not raised."[24]

When we reflect on the significance of glossolalia as it occurred among the prophets of the Cevennes, we note many similarities between them and the second-century Montanists. We wonder to what extent these experiences were hallucinatory, since hallucinations are not uncommon in times of stress and danger. As far as their speaking with tongues is concerned, Cutten remarks, ". . . We can see

23 Cutten, *op. cit.*, pp. 48-60; *Enc. Brit.*, IV, 705-706.
24 Warfield, *op. cit.*, pp. 129-30.

nothing in this or in similar cases which cannot be explained by known psychological laws."[25]

8. *The Jansenists.*

It is often said that there was some tongue-speaking among the Jansenists of eighteenth-century France. The *Britannica* article on Jansenism, however, explains that tongue-speaking was done by the more extravagant members of the group, who were eventually disowned by the more reputable Jansenists.[26]

9. *The Catholic Apostolic Church.*

A more extended manifestation of glossolalia appeared in the nineteenth century in the so-called Catholic Apostolic Church, founded by Edward Irving (1792-1834). Glossolalia began in this group when two people in Scotland started to speak in unknown tongues. Irving, who was then pastor of a London congregation, wanted these gifts for his church and hence began to pray for them. After a while glossolalia occurred within his group. Though at first he had intended to keep tongue-speaking a private exercise, Irving was soon permitting glossolalists to display their gift in public. After this, as Irving's close friend, Thomas Carlyle, used to say, his church services became pure bedlam.

At first it was thought that these tongues were actual foreign languages; Mary Campbell, the girl who had first begun to speak with tongues in Scotland, claimed that the tongue given to her was that of the Pelew Islands. This claim was, as one writer put it, "a safe statement . . . little likely to be authoritatively disputed."[27] Later, however,

---

[25] Cutten, *op. cit.*, p. 62. See his entire fourth chapter for further details.

[26] *Enc. Brit.*, XII, 892.

[27] Cutten, *op. cit.*, pp. 104-105.

the opinion was that the tongues were supernatural signs rather than specific languages.[28]

For a thorough evaluation of glossolalia among the "Irvingites," as the followers of Irving were often called, the reader is referred to Chapter Four of Warfield's *Miracles Yesterday and Today.* In this chapter Warfield tells about a certain Robert Baxter who joined Irving's church in 1831. For a time Baxter took an active part in the movement. But when prophecies that had been made failed to be fulfilled, Baxter's eyes were opened. He now openly broke with the movement, telling Irving of his conviction that "we had all been speaking by a lying spirit and not by the Spirit of the Lord."[29] Baxter even published a book in which he set forth his disillusionment with the supernatural gifts supposedly bestowed upon Irving's congregation.[30] Warfield goes on to say that even Mary Campbell later confessed that she had called some of her own impressions the voice of God.[31] We may conclude by observing that one does not receive a very favorable impression of tongue-speaking by studying the history of the Catholic Apostolic Church.

10. *Other Groups*

We could go on to note that there has been tongue-speaking among the Shakers and among the early Mormons (Article 7 of the Mormon Articles of Faith still claims the gift of tongues for Mormons today). We could also observe that there was tongue-speaking among some of the converts of Whitefield and Wesley, and that there was glossolalia in the Great Awakening in America and in

---

28 *Ibid.,* p. 105.
29 Warfield, *op. cit.,* pp. 142-43.
30 *Narrative of Facts Characterizing the Supernatural Manifestations in Members of Mr. Irving's Congregation* (London, 1833).
31 Warfield, *op. cit.,* p. 146.

the revivals in Scotland and Wales.[32] We might further take note of some instances of tongue-speaking in Russia and Armenia.[33] But enough of this history has been sketched to prove the point that glossolalia has occurred only occasionally in past years, and that it has been found to occur, not in the major segments of the historic Christian church but among minority groups, some of which were definitely heretical. Glossolalia is therefore not a part of the great tradition of historic Christianity, but is rather an isolated phenomenon which has occurred sporadically, under unusual circumstances.

The comparative silence of these many centuries of history as regards glossolalia ought to give serious pause to those who claim that the gift of tongues is one of the permanent gifts of the Spirit to the church. The voice of church history would seem to tell us that the Spirit has not continued to bestow this gift on God's people, though He has continued to guide His church into all the truth. Pentecostals counter that the reason this gift virtually disappeared from the church is that during these centuries God's people were sinning against God, [34] Christians failed to believe fully in all the promises of God,[35] and the love of many waxed cold.[36] The difficulty with this interpretation, however, is that it constitutes a wholesale indictment against 1800 years of church history. Must we honestly believe that no Christians of past ages — martyrs, missionaries, warriors, or saints — had the kind of faith, love, and dedication shown by Pentecostal believers today? Was

[32] Morton T. Kelsey, *Tongue Speaking*, pp. 57-59; *Enc. Brit.*, XXII, 289; Kurt Hutten, *Seher, Gruebler, Enthusiasten*, 6th ed., p. 479.

[33] Kelsey, *op. cit.*, pp. 65-68.

[34] Carl Brumback, *What Meaneth This?*, pp. 276, 280.

[35] Ralph M. Riggs, *The Spirit Himself*, p. 98; Donald Gee, *Concerning Spiritual Gifts*, p. 13.

[36] Gee, *op. cit.*, p. 10.

the entire history of the church from A.D. 100 to 1900 a history of apostasy?

The Pentecostal Movement

In October of 1900 a former Methodist minister, Charles F. Parham, opened a Bible college in Topeka, Kansas. Parham had been caught up in the holiness movement which was then at its height; he believed that sanctification was a second definite work of grace, which completely destroyed "inbred sin."[37] He was also convinced that after one had obtained real sanctification and the anointing that abides, there still remained a great outpouring of power which Christians should experience.[38]

Just before Christmas in 1900, Parham, who was leaving the school for three days, asked his students to learn from the Bible whether there is any evidence given for the baptism with the Holy Spirit — a blessing he felt the converted and sanctified believer ought still to receive.[39] When Parham returned, he was amazed to find that all forty of his students had come to the identical conclusion: "When the Pentecostal blessing fell, the indisputable proof on each occasion was that they spake with other tongues."[40] The group now actively began to seek a baptism with the Holy Spirit, the evidence of which was to be an ecstatic utterance in tongues.

On January 1, 1901 (and thus, as Pentecostals remind us, at the very beginning of the twentieth century), Miss Agnes Ozman, one of Parham's students, became the first

---

[37] Klaude Kendrick, *The Promise Fulfilled*, p. 40.

[38] *Ibid.*, p. 47.

[39] Note the idea behind this conception: there is a kind of third work of grace, in addition to conversion and sanctification.

[40] Robert L. Parham, compiler, *Selected Sermons of the Late Charles F. Parham and Sarah E. Parham* (published by the compiler, 1941), p. 58, as quoted in Kendrick, *op. cit.*, p. 51.

of this group to speak in tongues, after Parham had laid his hands upon her. This experience is called by Pentecostals the beginning of the modern Pentecostal revival.[41]

Soon other students began to speak with tongues, as did Parham himself. The latter became convinced that every Christian ought to receive the baptism with the Holy Spirit which he and his students had experienced, and ought to speak with tongues as proof that he had received this baptism. Parham now began to bring the "Pentecostal message" or "the full gospel message," as it was also called, to various other cities: Kansas City, Missouri; Lawrence, Kansas; El Dorado Springs, Missouri; Galena, Kansas; Joplin, Missouri; Orchard and Houston, Texas.[42] In 1905 Parham started a Bible school in Houston, Texas.

Among those who attended the Houston school and became convinced of the rightness of the Pentecost message was W. J. Seymour, a Negro holiness preacher. Around this time a Negro woman from Los Angeles, Neeley Terry by name, visited Houston, attended Mr. Seymour's church there, and received the baptism of the Holy Spirit and the gift of tongues. She was so impressed by Seymour that she persuaded the Los Angeles church to which she belonged to invite the brother to come and preach. Seymour's first message in Los Angeles, however, aroused such hostility that the visiting preacher found himself locked out of the church when he returned for the afternoon service. Undaunted, Seymour began to conduct meetings in a home. Here, on April 9, 1906, seven persons were baptized with the Holy Spirit and began to speak with tongues. These happenings attracted so much attention that the group soon moved to a building on Azusa Street, which had formerly been a church but had more recently been used as a livery stable.

41 Kendrick, *op. cit.*, p. 53.
42 *Ibid.*, pp. 54-63.

At this unpretentious place Seymour continued to conduct services — services which were attended by growing numbers of people from various denominations and races. These meetings continued for three years, and became the center of the Pentecostal movement. People came from all over the country to the Azusa Street Mission to receive the baptism with the Spirit and the evidential sign of tongues.[43]

There now followed years of rapid growth. The so-called Pentecostal revival spread to Chicago, Winnipeg, and New York City. Soon after 1906 the "full gospel" could be found on every continent. The movement continued to grow, until today it is estimated that there are at least 26 churches which consider themselves a part of the Pentecostal movement.[44]

Let us look briefly at some of the larger Pentecostal bodies in the United States. The largest and most influential of these is the *Assemblies of God,* with headquarters in Springfield, Missouri. As of April, 1965, their total membership in this country was in excess of 555,000; they had over 8,400 churches and over 10,000 ordained and 5,000 licensed ministers in the United States. Central Bible Institute in Springfield is their main training school, and the *Pentecostal Evangel* is their weekly paper. Some idea of the tremendous scope of their foreign missionary activity may be gathered from the fact that in April of 1965 they claimed to have 891 foreign missionaries, 15,105

43 *Ibid.,* pp. 64-68. To give but one example of the world-wide influence of the Azusa Street revival, T. Ḅ. Barratt, the founder of Norwegian Pentecostalism, who is regarded by most as the apostle of the Pentecostal movement in Europe, received the baptism of the Spirit and began to speak with tongues through the influence of the Azusa Street Mission (Nils Bloch-Hoell, *The Pentecostal Movement,* pp. 66-67, 75).

44 Kendrick, *op. cit.,* pp. 68-70; Kelsey, *op. cit.,* p. 84.

foreign churches and preaching points, and a foreign membership (including both adherents and communicants) of 1,472,766. This means that out of every four persons who are either members or "adherents" of the Assemblies of God, three are overseas, while only one is in the United States.[45]

The second largest Pentecostal church in the United States is the *Church of God in Christ.* This is a Negro church, founded by C. H. Mason and C. P. Jones. According to Kelsey, this group numbered over 400,000 in 1963, whereas it had only 31,000 members in 1936.[46] This is a holiness church, teaching that holiness is considered a prerequisite to salvation and to the baptism of the Spirit.

The third largest Pentecostal body is the *Church of God,* with headquarters in Cleveland, Tennessee. This is also the oldest Pentecostal church in the country, having been begun in 1886 in a revival in southeastern Tennessee led by Richard G. Spurling, Sr., and Richard G. Spurling, Jr. A. J. Tomlinson later became the general overseer of this church, but was impeached in 1923. This is also a holiness church, teaching that sanctification is subsequent to justification, and that the baptism with the Holy Ghost is subsequent to cleansing or sanctification.[47] According to figures received from this church in August of 1964, their total membership in the United States and Canada at that time was over 200,000; in these countries they had about 7,000 ministers (this figure probably includes licensed as well as ordained ministers) and about 3,500 churches. Their

[45] These figures were received from the denominational headquarters of the Assemblies of God in July of 1965.

[46] Kelsey, *op. cit.,* p. 86.

[47] Charles W. Conn, *Like a Mighty Army* (Cleveland, Tenn.: Church of God Publishing House, 1955), p. 311.

total world membership at that time, however, was about 400,000.[48]

Next in size is the *United Pentecostal Church*, which began when two bodies merged in 1945, and which is said by Kelsey to have about 175,000 members.[49] This is a so-called "Oneness" church: it denies that there are three Persons in the Trinity, claiming that Father, Son, and Holy Spirit are only one Person, and that that Person is Jesus Christ. This teaching is therefore a unique kind of unitarianism, centering in the Second Person instead of in the First; this Pentecostal type of unitarianism is sometimes also called the "Jesus Only" movement. People who had previously been baptized into the name of the Triune God had to be rebaptized into the name of Jesus when they joined this group. Most other Pentecostal bodies, the Assemblies of God in particular, have strongly repudiated this unitarian teaching. It might be of some interest to note that the United Pentecostal Church has a very strict moral code. It officially disapproves of such things as mixed bathing, make-up, worldly sports and amusements, television sets, and "women cutting their hair." In a booklet issued by the denomination entitled *The Hair Question,* fifteen reasons are given why women should have long hair.[50]

Another prominent Pentecostal church is the *International Church of the Foursquare Gospel,* founded in 1927 by Aimee Semple McPherson. This church also teaches that believers should receive the baptism of the Holy Spirit, and that this baptism will be attested by tongue-speaking. In 1965 this group claimed a total United States member-

[48] Letter from Charles W. Conn, First Assistant General Overseer of the Church of God, dated August 26, 1964.

[49] Kelsey, *op. cit.,* p. 85.

[50] Kendrick, *op. cit.,* pp. 174-75; see 171-75.

ship of 159,034, with 771 churches and 1,647 ordained and licensed ministers.[51] A folder on foreign mission work issued by the church in 1965 lists 1,368 national pastors and evangelists, 1,402 foreign churches and preaching stations, and 96,432 members and adherents in foreign countries.

The *Pentecostal Church of God in America* is another sizable Pentecostal body, whose headquarters are in Joplin, Missouri. A few years ago this church had about 100,000 members and 994 churches in the United States. At that time (about 1960) there were more than 300 mission churches in thirteen foreign countries.[52]

A Pentecostal holiness group with headquarters in Mobile, Alabama, is the *Apostolic Overcoming Holy Church of God*. This is also a Negro church. According to Bishop W. T. Phillips, founder and head of the church, in 1956 this group had 75,000 members in 300 churches.[53]

Another group which should be considered, if for no other reason than that Oral Roberts belongs to it, is the *Pentecostal Holiness Church*. Doctrinally, this is also a holiness group. Sanctification is considered an instantaneous second work of grace (though it is also held to be progressive). Baptism with the Holy Spirit is deemed an additional work of grace.[54] It is therefore interesting to note that figures submitted by the group in 1946 were broken down into three categories: 26,251 members, 8,043 saved, 3,179 sanctified, and 1,724 baptized with the Holy Spirit.[55] More recent statistics, however, indicate that, as

[51] Letter from the Office of the General Supervisor, International Church of the Foursquare Gospel, dated July 2, 1965.

[52] Frank S. Mead, *Handbook of Denominations in the United States* (New York: Abingdon Press, 1961; 2nd rev. ed.), pp. 172-73.

[53] *Ibid.*, p. 28.

[54] Kendrick, *op. cit.*, p. 184. Note that this church teaches three distinct works of grace.

[55] Elmer T. Clark, *The Small Sects in America* (New York: Abingdon Press, 1949; rev. ed.), pp. 107-108.

of July, 1956, the church claimed 60,665 members, 1,331 churches, and 2,446 ministers in the United States. The total world membership on that date was 84,915 with 85 missionaries serving outside the United States[56]

One more group should be mentioned, the *Pentecostal Assemblies of the World*. This is also a Negro church, which listed 50,000 members and 600 churches in 1959.[57] This church opposes secret societies, church festivals, the wearing of jewelry, attractive hosiery, bobbed hair, and bright ties.[58]

These, then, are the main Pentecostal bodies in the United States. There are a number of other groups, most of them smaller than the ones just described. Because of the rapid growth of Pentecostalism, not only in the States but also in foreign countries, this movement is often called the "Third Force in Christendom." There are many vigorous Pentecostal churches in such European countries as Norway, Sweden, Denmark, Finland, Switzerland, Russia, Italy, Germany, and England.[59] Pentecostalism is also strong in South America, particularly in Brazil.[60] Pentecostal churches have been very active in mission work; Bloch-Hoell, using figures for the year 1954, estimates that at that time the band of Pentecostal missionaries was at least three and a half times as large as "normal" within the Protestant world.[61] Though it is difficult to estimate how many people in the world could be called Pentecostal, it is certain that the figure would run well into the millions. Whereas Bloch-Hoell estimates that there are in the

[56] Letter from Bishop J. A. Synan, General Superintendent of the Pentecostal Holiness Church, received July 12, 1965.
[57] Kendrick, *op. cit.,* p. 4.
[58] Mead, *op. cit.,* p. 172.
[59] Nils Bloch-Hoell, *The Pentecostal Movement,* pp. 89-91.
[60] *Ibid.,* p. 91.
[61] *Ibid.,* p. 90.

neighborhood of six million Pentecostal followers in the world (if children are included), [62] John L. Sherrill suggests that there are 8,500,000 Pentecostals in the world, more than 2,000,000 of whom are in the United States.[63]

NEO-PENTECOSTALISM

One more phase of the history of this subject remains to be briefly explored — a phase which Russell T. Hitt has named Neo-Pentecostalism.[64] By this I mean the spread of glossolalia to the established churches. Previous to 1960 the phenomenon of tongue-speaking was pretty well confined to the Pentecostal churches; today, however, this is no longer the case.

It all began with Dennis Bennett, rector of St. Mark's Episcopal Church in Van Nuys, California, just outside of Los Angeles. Through the influence of a couple in a neighboring church he received the gift of tongues, and found it to be an exhilarating spiritual experience, the effects of which spilled over into his daily life. Soon there were about seventy persons in his congregation who had spoken in tongues, including some of the best-known members of the church. Since the congregation was divided on the issue, the Rev. Mr. Bennett resigned his rectorship on April 3, 1960. The publicity following upon his resignation spread the news of this new outburst of tongues far and wide.

Today glossolalia is being practiced by many Episcopalians. Frank Farrell reported in September of 1963 that some 2,000 Episcopalians were said to be speaking with tongues in Southern California alone.[65] Glossolalia has also spread to the Presbyterian Church — over 600 members

---

62 *Ibid.*

63 *They Speak With Other Tongues*, p. 15.

64 "The New Pentecostalism," *Eternity*, July, 1963.

65 Frank Farrell, "Outburst of Tongues: the New Penetration," *Christianity Today*, VII, 24 (Sept. 13, 1963), p. 3.

of Hollywood's First Presbyterian Church (the largest in the denomination) were also reported to be speaking with tongues.[66] Members of the Reformed Church of America have begun to speak with tongues; probably the best known of these is the Rev. Harald Bredesen, Pastor of the First Reformed Church of Mt. Vernon, New York. The Rev. Mr. Bredesen received the gift of tongues at a Pentecostal camp meeting in Green Lane, Pennsylvania, and since then has been actively propagandizing glossolalia. He is currently chairman of the Blessed Trinity Society, a group which is spearheading the Neo-Pentecostal movement, particularly by means of its quarterly, *Trinity*. It was Pastor Bredesen's visit to the Yale University campus that sparked an outburst of tongues there.

Glossolalia has also infiltrated the Lutheran churches. Probably the best-known Lutheran pastor who has received the gift is the Rev. Larry Christenson, pastor of Trinity Lutheran Church in San Pedro, California, who has done considerable writing on the subject. The movement has penetrated the Methodist Church; Morton Kelsey mentions a number of Methodist ministers who have received the gift of tongues and have been instrumental in giving it to others.[67] Tongue-speaking has also spread to the Baptist churches; Mr. Kelsey describes the experiences of two Baptist ministers who have received the gift, and quotes Dr. Francis Whiting, Director of the Department of Evangelism of the Michigan Baptist Convention (American Baptist), as saying that the salvation of the world lies in such charismatic gifts as the gift of tongues.[68]

In addition, it should be noted that glossolalia has cropped up in such smaller groups as the Inter-Varsity

---

[66] *Ibid.*
[67] *Op. cit.*, pp. 117-18.
[68] *Ibid.*, pp. 116-17.

Christian Fellowship, the Wycliffe Bible Translators, and the Navigators. It has also been reported at such well-known schools as Wheaton College, Westmont College, and Fuller Seminary.[69] Within the Neo-Pentecostal movement, in addition to the activities of the Blessed Trinity Society, there are meetings of small groups called Holy Spirit Fellowships, and there are Christian Advance meetings and conventions. An international organization called the Full Gospel Business Men's Fellowship International, with headquarters in Los Angeles, publishes three magazines: *Voice, Vision,* and *View.* This organization has a number of foreign directors in addition to those from the United States, and it has chapters in countries as far away as Australia and South Africa.

From all this it is quite evident that glossolalia today is spreading far beyond the Pentecostal churches. Though no figures are available, and though people who speak with tongues in the regular churches are often reluctant to admit that they do so, it is obvious that the number of people who have spoken with tongues or are still doing so outside the Pentecostal churches must be a sizable one. It is particularly the spread of glossolalia into the non-Pentecostal churches that makes the question of tongues such a live issue today.

[69] Frank Farrell, *loc. cit.,* p. 4.

2

The Significance of Tongue-Speaking
for Pentecostals

COMMON TO ALL PENTECOSTALS, AS WELL AS TO THOSE who are commonly called Neo-Pentecostals, is the practice of speaking with tongues. Before proceeding to evaluate this tongue-speaking, we must first understand what significance is ascribed to glossolalia by those who practice it.

It should be noted at the outset that there are differences of opinion among Pentecostals on the question of whether "entire sanctification" is necessary before one may receive the baptism of the Spirit which is accompanied by glossolalia.[1] By "entire sanctification" is meant the teaching that one is completely purified from indwelling sin in an instantaneous experience. At the beginning of the Pentecostal movement there was much emphasis on the importance of such instantaneous sanctification. It will be recalled that

[1] By "baptism of the Spirit," "baptism in the Spirit," "baptism with the Spirit," or "Spirit-baptism" (the terms will be used interchangeably) is meant the instantaneous experience in which a person, usually already a believer, is completely filled by the Holy Spirit, and thus receives full power for Christian service. All Pentecostal churches teach that believers should seek such a Spirit-baptism.

Charles F. Parham, at whose Bible school the Pentecostal movement first began, was a holiness preacher who believed in entire sanctification as a "second work of grace" after conversion. During the Los Angeles revival of 1906, in fact, many people claimed to have received entire sanctification, and it was frequently said that this blessing was necessary before one could receive the baptism of the Spirit.[2]

In the course of time, however, there came a shift in Pentecostal teaching. Though some Pentecostal bodies have continued to stress the necessity for entire sanctification as an experience which must precede the Spirit-baptism, so that Spirit-baptism is considered by them to be a third work of grace subsequent to regeneration (or conversion) and instantaneous sanctification,[3] most Pentecostal groups have abandoned this position.[4] The majority of Pentecostal churches now teach that sanctification is not an instantaneous experience, but a process which continues throughout life, even after one has received the baptism of the Spirit. By most Pentecostals, therefore, the baptism of the Spirit is considered a kind of "second work of grace" after regeneration.

Both groups of Pentecostals just described, however, agree that glossolalia is the initial evidence of Spirit-baptism. Since there is no difference of opinion among them on the point which now concerns us (that is, the significance of glossolalia), I shall ignore the difference of opinion on the question of entire sanctification in the ensuing discussion.

In attempting to assess the significance of glossolalia for those who practice it, we should further take account of another difference of opinion which exists among Pente-

[2] Bloch-Hoell, *The Pentecostal Movement,* p. 126.

[3] Among the Pentecostal groups still holding this position are the Church of God in Christ, the Church of God (Cleveland, Tennessee), and the Pentecostal Holiness Church.

[4] Bloch-Hoell, *op. cit.,* p. 131.

costals. Not all of them are agreed that glossolalia invariably accompanies the baptism of the Spirit. Some Pentecostals maintain that, though tongue-speaking is one of the evidences of Spirit-baptism, it is not necessarily the only evidence, and that therefore a person could have received the baptism of the Spirit without having spoken with tongues. Such prominent European Pentecostal leaders as T. B. Barratt of Norway and Lewi Pethrus of Sweden are willing to admit that, as an exception, the Spirit-baptism may occur without glossolalia.[5] J. E. Stiles, Jr., wrote in *Christianity Today* not long ago, "There is a growing minority among Full Gospel people who do not believe that tongues is the 'only' or 'necessary' evidence of the initial receiving of the Holy Spirit. We do accept that it is *an* evidence."[6] Nils Bloch-Hoell, whose historical study of the Pentecostal movement is the most thorough so far published, states:

> The dominant opinion of the Pentecostal Movement is that the Spirit baptism is accompanied by the speaking with tongues, but, at the same time, it allows, theoretically, the possibility of Spirit baptism without glossolalia.[7]

It would appear, therefore, that, though a minority of Pentecostals would grant the possibility of Spirit-baptism without glossolalia, the majority would view a Spirit-baptism as incomplete or inconclusive without glossolalia.[8]

Though the reader should keep in mind the fact that there are Pentecostals who do not go along entirely with the position of the majority, I shall set forth the majority view as typical of the Pentecostal movement. In presenting this

---

5 *Ibid.*, p. 131.

6 Issue of Nov. 8, 1963, p. 17.

7 *Op. cit.*, pp. 131-32.

8 At this point we are considering only the position of members of Pentecostal churches. The question of the views of Neo-Pentecostals on this matter will be taken up later in the chapter.

majority view, I shall reproduce, as far as possible, the position held by the Assemblies of God, the largest Pentecostal church in the United States, and probably the most influential Pentecostal body in the world.

The Assemblies of God have set forth their main doctrinal tenets in what they call their *Statement of Fundamental Truths,* comprising 16 articles. Article 7 of this Statement reads as follows:

> All believers are entitled to and should ardently expect and earnestly seek the promise of the Father, the baptism in the Holy Ghost and fire, according to the command of our Lord Jesus Christ. This was the normal experience of all in the early Christian Church. With it comes the endue-ment of power for life and service, the bestowment of the gifts and their uses in the work of the ministry (Luke 24:49; Acts 1:4, 8; I Cor. 12:1-31). This experience is distinct from and subsequent to the experience of the new birth (Acts 8:12-17; 10:44-46; 11:14-16; 15:7-9). With the baptism in the Holy Ghost come such experiences as an overflowing fullness of the Spirit (John 7:37-39; Acts 4:8), a deepened reverence for God (Acts 2:43; Heb. 12:28), an intensified consecration to God and dedication to His work (Acts 2:42), and a more active love for Christ, for His Word and for the lost (Mark 16:20).

Article 8 makes the following assertions:

> The Baptism of believers in the Holy Ghost is witnessed by the initial physical sign of speaking with other tongues as the Spirit of God gives them utterance (Acts 2:4). The speaking in tongues in this instance is the same in essence as the gift of tongues (I Cor. 12:4-10, 28), but different in purpose and use.[9]

9 Quoted from . . . *In the Last Days* . . ., An Early History of the Assemblies of God (Springfield: Assemblies of God International Headquarters, 1962), p. 31. The *Statement of Fundamental Truths* was revised late in 1961; the above quotations are from the revised text.

Putting these two articles together, we arrive at the following conclusions:

(1) All believers should seek the baptism in the Holy Ghost.

(2) This Spirit-baptism is different from and subsequent to the experience of the new birth.

(3) This Spirit-baptism bestows power for life and service, greater consecration, and more active love for Christ, for His Word, and for the lost.

(4) The initial physical sign of this Spirit-baptism is speaking with other tongues.

(5) This initial physical sign, though the same in essence as the gift of tongues spoken of in I Corinthians 12, is different in purpose and use.

For the Assemblies of God, therefore — and their position on this matter is typical of Pentecostals in general — glossolalia is so important that every believer should try to exercise it, as the initial evidence of that Spirit-baptism which all must seek to obtain. I quote from a prominent Assemblies of God author:

> ONE experience must be received by all who would enter the kingdom — the new birth. . . . In like manner, all believers are commanded to receive ONE experience — the baptism or filling with the Spirit. Again, physical, emotional and intellectual reactions are as varied as the recipients, but again ONE evidence uniformly accompanies the experience — *The witness of the Spirit through us in other tongues!*[10]

10 Carl Brumback, *What Meaneth This?*, p. 248 (the italics are Brumback's). This book was recommended to me by Russell Spittler, a member of the faculty of Central Bible Institute, as one of the two best books setting forth Assembly of God teachings on glossolalia. The other book mentioned was Ralph M. Riggs, *The Spirit Himself.* Other Pentecostal bodies have not issued doctrinal studies as thorough as these. These two books, therefore, shall be heavily relied on as setting forth Pentecostal teachings on glossolalia and Spirit-baptism.

Ralph M. Riggs, another Assemblies of God writer, in fact, gives ten reasons why we should receive Spirit-baptism shortly after conversion.[11] The importance of glossolalia for Pentecostals is further indicated by the following statement from Carl Brumback: "It is our sincere belief that without this evidence [namely, that of glossolalia] there can be no fully Scriptural baptism with the Holy Ghost."[12] Glossolalia should therefore be sought by every Christian, not for its own sake, but as evidence that one has received the baptism in the Holy Ghost.

What, now, is this Spirit-baptism which is said to be subsequent to and distinct from the new birth? It means the coming of the Holy Spirit into one's life as a Person in His own name and right. Ralph Riggs describes the experience as follows:

> As the Spirit of Christ, He had come at conversion, imparting the Christ-life, revealing Christ, and making Him real. At the Baptism in the Spirit, He Himself in His own person comes upon and fills the waiting believer. This experience is as distinct from conversion as the Holy Spirit is distinct from Christ. His coming to the believer at the Baptism is the coming of the Third Person of the Trinity, in addition to the coming of Christ, which takes place at conversion.[13]

[11] *The Spirit Himself,* pp. 82-83.

[12] *Op. cit.,* p. 188. Note also the following statement, which occurs in a footnote on p. 32: "It is not the prerogative of any one author to interpret infallibly the doctrinal beliefs of the entire Pentecostal Movement concerning tongues. Nevertheless, we feel that in most instances this volume will set forth only that which is generally believed by the Movement; and in those instances where we may advance a personal conviction not generally accepted by the Movement, we shall be careful to designate it as such." There is no indication on p. 188 that the "sincere belief" quoted above is not generally accepted by the Pentecostal Movement. The thrust of the context, in fact, is that this belief is one which all, or certainly most, Pentecostals hold in common.

[13] *Op. cit.,* pp. 79-80.

Does this mean, now, that one does not receive the Holy Spirit in any sense at the time of conversion? On the contrary, every Christian does have the Holy Spirit, since the Spirit must bring him into contact with Christ and since the Spirit must bring about regeneration.[14] But only after the Spirit-baptism does the third Person of the Trinity take definite control in His own right, and does He dispense the full complement of His gifts.[15] In short, though one receives certain fruits of the power of the Holy Spirit at the time of regeneration or conversion, he does not receive the Spirit as a Person who fills his life completely until the time of the Baptism in the Holy Ghost. Of this Spirit-baptism, glossolalia is the initial evidence.

On what Scriptural material is this teaching based? Chiefly on a study of the passages in the book of Acts which describe certain groups as speaking with tongues as the Holy Spirit fell or came upon them. We shall be examining these Scriptural data in greater detail later on.

It will be remembered that Pentecostals distinguish between glossolalia as the initial evidence of Spirit-baptism and as a gift which the recipient may continue to exercise. In this way they account for the obvious fact that not everyone at Corinth had the gift of tongues.[16] In brief, their position is this: all who receive the Spirit-baptism must speak with tongues as the initial physical evidence of this baptism. Not all who receive this evidence, however, continue to exercise the gift of tongues.[17]

14 *Ibid.*, pp. 79, 118.

15 *Ibid.*, pp. 118-19. Cf. Morton T. Kelsey, *Tongue Speaking*, p. 78: "The Christian who receives spiritual baptism and speaks in tongues then enters into a charismatic life in which he is open to receive all of the other gifts of the Spirit." Kelsey is here reproducing Pentecostal teaching.

16 Brumback, *op. cit.*, pp. 261-72.

17 According to Bloch-Hoell, the Pentecostal movement in its early stages did not distinguish between glossolalia as a sign of the Spirit-

The gift of tongues, furthermore, is twofold in its operation: devotional and congregational. As a devotional exercise, tongues may be used as a means for praying, giving thanks, or singing. Through this use of the gift one edifies himself.[18] The other use of the gift is congregational. Tongues should be used in church services — Brumback states that it is a good thing for the preacher to be occasionally interrupted by an utterance in tongues, though he does not encourage constant interruption.[19] Donald Gee, another Assembly of God writer, reflecting on the differences between Pentecostal and ordinary Protestant church services, puts the matter rather quaintly: "Better a little disorder and the Lord working than the apparent 'order' of the graveyard and of death."[20] When tongues are used in a church service, however, they must be interpreted; hence Pentecostals speak of the gift of interpretation as an additional gift. If there is no interpreter, the tongue-speaker should keep silent in the church.[21]

It may be of interest to ask at this point: what, according to Pentecostals, are these tongues like? Are they real human languages, or mere ecstatic utterances which bear no resemblance to languages actually spoken on earth? To answer this question I must first briefly reproduce Pentecostal

---

baptism and as a gift of grace. It was generally believed at that time, he continues, that glossolalia in connection with Spirit-baptism was a permanent gift of grace. Later, however, the distinction described above was introduced; this distinction is now commonly made by most, if not all, Pentecostals (*op. cit.*, p. 142).

18 Brumback, *op cit.*, pp. 291-98.

19 *Ibid.*, pp. 327-28. On the congregational use of tongues, see also pp. 299-317.

20 *Concerning Spiritual Gifts*, p. 96. For a further description of Pentecostal services, see Klaude Kendrick, *The Promise Fulfilled*, pp. 70-72; and Riggs, *op. cit.*, pp. 176-86.

21 Brumback, *op. cit.*, pp. 301-311. It is implied in this discussion that not all Pentecostal churches observe the restrictions on tongue-speaking laid down by Paul in I Cor. 14:27-28.

teachings on the tongues described in Scripture. Pentecostals are pretty well agreed that the tongues spoken on Pentecost Day were actual languages, since Luke says that every man heard the disciples speaking in his own language.[22] As far as the glossolalia at Corinth is concerned, Brumback contends that, though there is a difference between the tongues in Acts and those in Corinth as regards their purpose and operation, there is no difference between them as regards their nature: in other words, in Corinth as well as in Jerusalem the tongues were actual foreign languages spoken by people who had no previous training in those languages.[23]

On the basis of his view of glossolalia as it is described in Scripture, Brumback contends that glossolalia today is not the speaking of a heavenly language unknown to man but the speaking of actual human languages that are, however, unknown to the persons speaking them;[24] he even claims that there are cases on record where glossolalic utterances have been identified as actual languages by both Pentecostal and non-Pentecostal believers.[25] Brumback admits that sometimes present-day glossolalia is not in a genuine language, but is mere gibberish; such instances, however, he classifies as fraudulent attempts to imitate the genuine gift of tongues.[26] Donald Gee, a British Pentecostal writer, agrees that glossolalia today is the speaking of genuine foreign languages.[27] It would appear, then, to be the common Pentecostal position that glossolalia as practiced today is the speaking of actual foreign languages by per-

[22] *Ibid.*, p. 20. Riggs even suggests that 15 different languages were spoken by the disciples on that day (*op. cit.*, p. 86).

[23] Brumback, *op. cit.*, pp. 249-50, 263-64.

[24] *Ibid.*, pp. 295-96.

[25] *Ibid.*, p. 113.

[26] *Ibid.*, p. 112, n. 1.

[27] *Op. cit.*, pp. 57, 61, 62, 96.

sons who have never studied the languages in which they speak and who do not understand them at the time of speaking.

It should be observed, however, that not all Pentecostals agree on this point. Pentecostals have told me in private conversations that present-day glossolalia could be either the speaking of actual foreign languages, or the speaking of an ecstatic language which has no counterpart among human languages. It is also significant that at least one Assembly of God writer does not share the view that glossolalia today is always in actual foreign languages. Stanley H. Frodsham, in a book which is still recommended in the current catalog of the Gospel Publishing House, the official publishing agency of the Assemblies of God, has this to say about the gift of tongues:

> The child of God is privileged to have speech with God and no man understands this secret speech, for the saint is allowed to speak in the language of Divinity — a language unknown to humanity. . . . The humblest saint can enjoy supernatural converse with Him who made the worlds, in a language not understood by man, or by the devil either.[28]

We go on now to ask whether the view of Neo-Pentecostals about the significance and value of glossolalia is the same as that of the Pentecostals just described. This question is difficult to answer because there is no single authoritative theological interpretation which is binding on all Neo-Pentecostals. It should be noted, however, that Neo-Pentecostalism received its initial impetus from the Pentecostals, many of the leaders of the former movement having received the gift of tongues in Pentecostal

---

[28] *With Signs Following*, 1926 ed., pp. 242-43. The same statement is found in the 1946 ed. of this book, pp. 268-69.

meetings or through the influence of Pentecostals. Historically, therefore, Neo-Pentecostalism grew out of Pentecostalism.

It has already been noted that there is some difference of opinion among members of Pentecostal churches on the question of whether glossolalia invariably accompanies the baptism of the Spirit. We find a similar difference of opinion among Neo-Pentecostals. Some Neo-Pentecostals believe that glossolalia is one of the evidences of having received the baptism of the Spirit, but not necessarily the only evidence or the indispensable evidence. To cite an example, the Rev. Larry Christenson, pastor of the Trinity Lutheran Church of San Pedro, California, and a leader in the Neo-Pentecostal movement, is not at all ready to say that everyone who receives the baptism of the Spirit will speak in tongues, so that if a person has not spoken in tongues one is justified in concluding that that person has not received the Spirit-baptism.[29] He grants, however, that the book of Acts gives us a helpful pattern to follow in our lives today: namely, receiving the Spirit as an instantaneous experience, which is accompanied by speaking with tongues.[30] He therefore goes on to say:

> To consummate one's experience of receiving the Holy Spirit by speaking in tongues gives it an objectivity; I believe this objectivity has a definite value for one's *continued walk in the Spirit,* for speaking in tongues seems to have a definite bearing on the "pruning" and "refining" which a Christian must go through.[31]

[29] "Speaking in Tongues," *Trinity,* II, 4 (Transfiguration, 1963), p. 15.

[30] *Ibid.* Note that here "receiving the Spirit" means being baptized with the Spirit. Both Pentecostals and Neo-Pentecostals often use the expression "receiving" as a synonym for Spirit-baptism.

[31] *Ibid.*

According to Christenson, therefore, glossolalia, though highly valuable, is not the indispensable evidence of having received Spirit-baptism.

According to Morton T. Kelsey, an Episcopal rector who has written a recent book on tongue-speaking, the Rev. Tod Ewald, rector of the Episcopal Church in Corte Madera, California, shares Christenson's views on tongues.[32] Kelsey goes on to say that, in his opinion, the majority of tongue-speakers in the older Protestant denominations share Pastor Christenson's views on tongues and on the experience of the Holy Spirit: namely, that tongues are *a* sign of the baptism of the Spirit, but not *the indispensable* sign of that event.[33] If Kelsey is correct, this would mean that the majority view among Neo-Pentecostals differs from the majority view among Pentecostals.

I am not certain, however, that Mr. Kelsey is correct in his judgment. I have come across a number of statements by prominent Neo-Pentecostal leaders affirming that glossolalia is not just *a possible* evidence, but *the* evidence of the baptism with the Holy Spirit. For example, Robert Frost, professor of biology at Westmont College, writing in *Trinity* magazine, states that, just as a confession of faith is the outward confirmation of conversion, so speaking with tongues is the outward evidence of the baptism with the Holy Spirit (which he calls "the gift of God's Spirit in His fulness").[34] In an earlier issue of the same periodical the Rev. Edwin B. Stube, Vicar of St. Lawrence's, Sidney, Montana, and a director of the Blessed Trinity Society, asserts:

[32] *Op. cit.*, p. 127.
[33] *Ibid.*
[34] "What Meaneth This?", *Trinity*, II, 3 (Eastertide, 1963), p. 16.

> In the New Testament, *the standard sign or evidence of the Baptism* of the Holy Spirit is that of speaking with other tongues as the Spirit gives utterance. . . . It is clearly God's intention that all believers should receive the Baptism of the Holy Spirit with the sign which the New Testament indicates [namely, the sign of tongue-speaking].[35]

Jean Stone, another director of the Blessed Trinity Society, and the editor of *Trinity* magazine, has this to say about glossolalia in an editorial: "When a believer is baptized with the Holy Spirit we believe he will speak with new tongues as the Spirit gives utterance and that this empowerment (signified by the new language) is an empowerment for service."[36] In this same editorial Mrs. Stone quotes an official statement made by the Board of Directors of the Blessed Trinity Society at its March, 1963, meeting. The fourth paragraph of that statement reads as follows:

> We believe that when a Christian receives the Baptism with the Holy Spirit, promised by Jesus (Acts 1:5, 8), the Holy Spirit confirms it with a supernatural ability to speak in a language unknown to the speaker.[37]

The members of the Board of Directors listed in the issue of the magazine in which the above statement appeared are the following: the Rev. Harald Bredesen, the Rev. David J. du Plessis, the Rev. Tod W. Ewald, Donald D. Stone, the Rev. William T. Sherwood, Jean Stone, the Rev. Edwin B. Stube.[38] It would appear that a statement by

---

35 "The Ministries of the Holy Spirit in the Church," *Trinity*, I, 3 (Eastertide, 1962), p. 42.

36 *Trinity*, II, 3 (Eastertide, 1963), p. 34.

37 *Ibid.* It will be noted that there is no qualifying expression like "usually," "generally," or "in most cases."

38 *Ibid.*, p. 1. Note that among those who apparently agreed with this statement is the Rev. Tod Ewald, whom Mr. Kelsey, as we saw, lists as being of a different opinion.

the Board of Directors of the Blessed Trinity Society would come as close as one could reasonably expect to an official pronouncement concerning the views of Neo-Pentecostals.

I would therefore conclude that, with possible exceptions, the dominant position of Neo-Pentecostalism on the significance of glossolalia is the same as that of the Pentecostals: tongue-speaking is the necessary evidence that one has received the baptism of the Spirit.

It will be granted that most Neo-Pentecostals do not wish to encourage tongue-speaking at the regular Sunday services of their churches, but prefer to exercise glossolalia in their private devotions or in small prayer groups.[39] It may also be freely admitted that tongue-speaking among Neo-Pentecostals is often much less emotionally charged than it is in many Pentecostal church services or weekday meetings.[40] These differences, however, do not affect the basic point now under discussion: the significance of glossolalia as evidence of Spirit-baptism. On this point it would appear that most Neo-Pentecostals agree with most Pentecostals.

[39] Kelsey, *op. cit.*, p. 126; Frank Farrell, "Outburst of Tongues," *Christianity Today*, VII (Sept. 13, 1963), p. 6.
[40] Kelsey, *op. cit.*, p. 145; Farrell, *loc. cit.*, p. 6.

3

A Biblical Evaluation of Tongue-Speaking

IT WILL, OF COURSE, BE GRANTED THAT THERE IS MUCH which the church can learn from both Pentecostalism and Neo-Pentecostalism. Though this point will be more fully discussed in Chapter 5, let me say here that there is in the church today a crying need for a greater infilling with the Holy Spirit, for greater fervor in our worship, and for greater warmth in our testimony. All of us who call ourselves Christians want to live more Spirit-filled lives. All of us want to welcome whatever will help us more fully to walk by the Spirit.

Yet our main concern as Bible-believing Christians must always be to remain true to the teachings of God's Word. We may not begin with a certain type of religious experience, and then proceed to build a doctrine upon it. Our doctrines must be based, not on experience, but on the teachings of Scripture. We must therefore subject Pentecostalism in both its older and newer forms to the test of Scripture. Hence I propose in this chapter to give a Biblical evaluation of the teachings of both Pentecostals and Neo-Pentecostals on tongue-speaking.[1]

It should, of course, be remembered that not every Pentecostal and not every Neo-Pentecostal subscribes wholly to the position on tongue-speaking that has been sketched in Chapter 2 above. In making this Biblical evaluation, however, I have assumed that the position on tongue-speaking maintained by the majority of Pentecostals and Neo-Pentecostals may safely be held to be typical of the movement as a whole.

In conducting this Biblical evaluation I shall take up, in turn, various groups of Scripture passages which have been adduced by Pentecostals in their attempt to find Biblical support for glossolalia.

1. *Passages from the prophets adduced by Pentecostals as pointing to tongue-speaking.*

Two frequently cited passages come into consideration here. Pentecostals find a prediction of tongue-speaking in Isaiah 28:11, 12. In the King James Version this passage reads as follows:

> For with stammering lips and another tongue will he speak to this people.

[1] In reproducing these teachings I shall, however, rely heavily on Pentecostal writers, especially on such men as Carl Brumback and Ralph M. Riggs, since these men speak representatively for the Pentecostal Movement, and since they have set forth Pentecostal teachings in greater detail than has been done by other writers. As we have seen, the majority position of Neo-Pentecostalism on the significance of glossolalia is the same as that of Pentecostalism; one generally finds in Neo-Pentecostal literature the same types of Scripture passages and the same basic interpretation of these passages that one finds in Pentecostal literature. Hence I believe that a treatment of the Pentecostal position on tongues will also serve as a treatment of the Neo-Pentecostal position.

To whom he said, This is the rest wherewith ye may cause the weary to rest; and this is the refreshing: yet they would not hear.

Usually, when quoting this passage, Pentecostals leave off the last clause, "yet they would not hear." They then proceed to interpret the passage as predicting the bestowal of the gift of tongues on the church, adding that through this gift, according to the prophet, rest will be granted to the people of God.[2] What is forgotten, however, is that, when seen in the light of the context, the passage clearly predicts the coming of the Assyrians upon the people of Israel, as a punishment for their disobedience. Verse 12 refers to previous prophetic warnings which had been disregarded; hence this punishment is now on its way: "To whom he said, This is the rest wherewith ye may cause the weary to rest . . . yet they would not hear." To assert that the rest here spoken of is a result of speaking with tongues, as our Pentecostal friends do, is to twist the meaning of the text. Paul's use of this passage in I Corinthians 14:21, furthermore, does not support the Pentecostal interpretation. For Paul's point is not that the speaking in strange tongues brings rest, but rather that, as in Old Testament times, so now: this type of speaking leaves people unbelieving, leaves their hearts hardened: "not even thus will they hear me, saith the Lord."

Another prophetic passage often adduced by Pentecostals is found in the second chapter of Joel's prophecy. In the latter part of this chapter there occurs the promise of the outpouring of the Spirit on all flesh which Peter quoted

2 Carl Brumback, *What Meaneth This?*, p. 294; Ralph M. Riggs, *The Spirit Himself*, pp. 65, 78, 162; Stanley H. Frodsham, *With Signs Following* (1946 ed.), pp. 263-64; Ernest S. Williams, *Systematic Theology*, III, 49.

on Pentecost Day. From this part of the chapter Pentecostal authors go back to the 23rd verse to find a reference
to former and latter rain:

> Be glad then, ye children of Zion, and rejoice in the Lord
> your God: for he hath given you the former rain moder-
> ately, and he will cause to come down for you the rain,
> the former rain, and the latter rain in the first month.

This verse, now, is linked with James 5:7, 8, which reads
as follows:

> Be patient therefore, brethren, unto the coming of the
> Lord. Behold, the husbandman waiteth for the precious
> fruit of the earth, and hath long patience for it, until he
> receive the early and latter rain.
> Be ye also patient; stablish your hearts: for the coming
> of the Lord draweth nigh.

Since the James passage refers to the second coming
of the Lord, it is ingeniously assumed that the "latter
rain" designates an event which must immediately precede Christ's return. Rain must somehow tie in with the
outpouring of the Spirit predicted by Joel. So the conclusion is obvious: the "former rain" or "early rain" must
refer to the outburst of tongues on Pentecost Day and in
the early church, whereas the "latter rain" must designate
the tongues movement of recent times.[3] One frequently
finds Pentecostals referring to the Pentecostal revival which
began in 1901 as the "latter-rain movement." An implication of this term, seen in the light of the Joel and
James passages, is that the Pentecostal movement is a
sign of the nearness of Christ's return and of the end of
the world. This interpretation of "former rain" and

---

[3] P. C. Nelson, *Bible Doctrines*, p. 80; Riggs, *op. cit.*, pp. 93-94;
Donald Gee, *Concerning Spiritual Gifts*, p. 99; Brumback, *op. cit.*,
pp. 114, 281.

"latter rain," however, is completely without Biblical support, as the most elementary study of these passages in context will reveal.[4]

2. Passages adduced to show that tongue-speaking was to remain in the church.

Carl Brumback, in his *What Meaneth This?*, meets the argument that glossolalia was temporary and was not intended to continue in the church by pointing to two passages which, so he claims, teach that God did intend tongues to continue. The first of these is Mark 16:17-18. In the King James Version this passage reads as follows:

> And these signs shall follow them that believe; In my name shall they cast out devils; they shall speak with new tongues;
> They shall take up serpents; and if they drink any deadly thing, it shall not hurt them; they shall lay hands on the sick, and they shall recover.

Here Jesus makes it very plain — so Brumback argues — that tongues are to remain in the church: "These signs shall follow them that believe . . . they shall speak with new tongues."[5]

There is, however, a real question about the genuineness of this passage. The longer ending of Mark, in which this verse occurs, is missing in the two oldest uncials, the Vaticanus and the Sinaiticus, both dating from the fourth

---

[4] In Joel the former rain and the latter rain are simply symbolic figures to picture the blessings of the Lord which will follow the plagues and disasters described in the early chapters of the book. In the James passage the figure of the husbandman waiting for the early and latter rain is used to teach patience while waiting for the return of the Lord.

[5] *Op. cit.*, pp. 61-69. Cf. Riggs, *op. cit.*, p. 162; Nelson, *op. cit.*, pp. 97-98; Frodsham, *op. cit.* (1946 ed.) , p. 268.

century A.D.[6] Though this longer ending is found in a number of later manuscripts of this Gospel, other manuscripts have a shorter ending; at least one uncial (Codex Regius, or Manuscript L) has both the shorter and the longer ending. There is also internal evidence against the genuineness of the longer ending: certain words and constructions are used in it which are either not commonly used in Mark or not used at all in Mark. In the light of all these facts, it seems highly unlikely that the longer ending of Mark was part of the original Gospel. Most evangelical commentators, therefore, regard the longer ending of Mark as not genuine, including so noted a conservative scholar as the late Professor Ned Stonehouse of Westminster Seminary.[7] It is therefore hardly correct and certainly not gracious to suggest, as Brumback does, that those who have their doubts about the genuineness of Mark 16:15-20 are like modernists who remove from the Bible whatever passages are distasteful to them![8] This is not a question of taste or distaste, but simply a question of manuscript evidence.

Suppose, however, that we assume for a moment that Mark 16:17-18 may still be authoritative for us (perhaps by accepting it as Scripture even while agreeing that it was probably written by someone other than Mark). Even then we would have difficulties with this passage. It will be recalled that the passage not only speaks of new tongues but also of taking up serpents and drinking deadly poison.

---

[6] Uncials are the oldest major manuscripts of the New Testament. The three uncials generally considered most important for the establishment of the text of the New Testament are the two mentioned above and Alexandrinus, which dates from the 5th century A.D. Of these three, only Alexandrinus has the longer ending.

[7] *The Witness of Matthew and Mark to Christ* (Grand Rapids: Eerdmans, 1958), p. 82.

[8] *Op. cit.*, p. 62.

Pentecostals are not particularly eager to advise their people to begin picking up serpents or drinking poison to prove that they are true believers.[9] How, then, do they get around the thought that the last-named two signs also still follow those that believe? Brumback contends that the reason these miraculous signs have disappeared from the church is lack of faith among God's people.[10] The trouble with this explanation, however, is that according to Brumback the Pentecostals now have the faith that the church failed to exercise during previous centuries, and hence they now speak with tongues.[11] But then we ask, Why don't they also take up serpents and drink poison? The only answer Brumback gives to this question is to suggest that the taking up of serpents without harm was done in the early church "accidentally, of course," and that being preserved from deadly poison is to happen only when such poison has been "inadvertently taken or administered by an enemy."[12] As we examine the Greek text of Mark 16:18, however, we find that, though the statement about drinking poison is put in a conditional form ("if they drink any deadly thing, it shall not hurt them"), the statement about taking up serpents is not put in conditional form, but is in the future indicative: "they shall take up serpents," as is the statement about tongues: "they shall speak with new tongues." According to the text, therefore, these signs shall follow them that believe: they shall

---

9 There are, however, snake-handling cults in certain southern states by whom the reference to serpents in Mark 16:18 is interpreted quite literally. Poisonous snakes are released at their church services, worshipers permitting themselves to be bitten by the serpents as a test of faith (Elmer T. Clark, *The Small Sects in America*, pp. 98-99).

10 Brumback, *op. cit.*, pp. 83-87; cf. Riggs, *op. cit.*, p. 98.

11 Brumback, *op. cit.*, pp. 276-81.

12 *Ibid.*, p. 84.

speak with new tongues, and they shall take up serpents. If the speaking with new tongues is to be taken as a sign which confirms believers in their faith, why must we not further conclude that taking up serpents is also to function as such a sign? There is as much reason for accepting the one sign as the other, since in both cases the Greek verb is in the future indicative: *lalēsousin . . . arousin.* If Mark 16:17-18 be authoritative Scripture, why should not all Pentecostal churches become snake-handling cults?

For the reasons given, therefore, I do not believe that Mark 16:17-18 proves that the gift of tongues is still in the church today.

Another passage adduced by Brumback to prove that glossolalia was intended to remain in the church is I Corinthians 12:28.[13] This passage reads as follows:

> And God hath set some in the church, first apostles, secondarily prophets, thirdly teachers, after that miracles, then gifts of healings, helps, governments, diversities of tongues.

I would agree with Brumback that these words were intended, not just for the church at Corinth, but for the church of all time — the reference to apostles proves this, for surely God did not give apostles only to the Corinthian church. Brumback goes on to argue that, since "diversities of tongues" are mentioned among the gifts God has given to His church, the gift of tongues must still be in the church today.[14]

Does the passage prove this? Not conclusively. For the text begins by saying that God has set apostles in the church. Apostles, however, are no longer with us, as Brum-

13 *Ibid.,* p. 69.
14 *Ibid.,* pp. 69-71.

back himself admits.[15] Can we be certain, then, that all the gifts mentioned in this verse are still in the church today? There are, furthermore, some puzzling expressions in this verse. What is meant by "miracles" (*dunameis*)? Are these still in the church today? Our Pentecostal brothers contend that gifts of healings (*charismata iamatōn*) are still in the church. But can we be sure of this? What is meant by "helps" (*antilēmpseis*)? What is meant by "governments" (*kubernēseis*)? Can we be sure that these gifts are still present today? Leon Morris points to the inadequacy of our understanding of the exact nature of some of these gifts. He says, "We may make . . . conjectures. . . . But when we boil it all down, we know nothing about these gifts or their possessors. They have vanished without leaving visible trace."[16] I am not contending, now, that I can prove from this passage that tongues are no longer in the church; I am only saying that Pentecostals cannot prove with finality from this text that all the gifts mentioned here are still in the church today.[17]

3. Passages adduced to prove that there is a Spirit-baptism distinct from and subsequent to regeneration, of which tongue-speaking is the initial physical evidence.

Here we come close to the heart of Pentecostal teaching.

[15] *Ibid.*, p. 70. It is generally agreed by interpreters that the word "apostles" here is not used in the wider sense, in which it may apply to such individuals as Barnabas (Acts 14:14) or Andronicus and Junias (Rom. 16:7), but in the narrower sense in which it applies only to the twelve and Paul. See the commentaries of Calvin, Hodge, Lenski, Grosheide (*New International Commentary*), and cf. K. H. Rengstorf in *Theological Dict. of the New Testament*, ed. Gerhard Kittel, trans. G. W. Bromiley, I, 423.

[16] *Spirit of the Living God* (Chicago: Inter-Varsity Press, 1960), p. 63.

[17] For a more thorough discussion of the question of the permanence of the miraculous gifts, including glossolalia, see Chapter 4.

This is the central doctrine that distinguishes Pentecostal churches from other Protestant bodies, and that, as we have seen, is also held by most Neo-Pentecostals. Because of their teaching on the baptism with the Holy Ghost, there is in Pentecostal churches a tremendous drive to "break through" or to "receive" or to "get the baptism." Sometimes people agonize for years to receive this gift. When I was selling Bibles in Louisiana as a seminary student, I once talked to a woman who was a member of a Pentecostal Church.

"What about your husband?" I asked her.

"Oh, he's a seeker," was the reply.

"A seeker? What do you mean?"

"He's seeking the Holy Spirit."

"You mean," I continued, "that he's not a believer?"

"Of course he's a believer."

"He doesn't go to church?"

"Of course he goes to church — every Sunday."

"Well, why do you call him a seeker?"

"Because he doesn't have the baptism of the Spirit yet."

"How long has he been a seeker?"

"Oh, about ten years."

One can imagine the psychological and spiritual tensions which a teaching of this sort creates. When one does not receive the baptism of the Spirit at once, he tries a little harder. When after several attempts one still does not receive it, he feels badly frustrated. I have read of instances where people have become mentally ill because they failed to "receive." Pentecostals teach that, though one may be saved without this Spirit-baptism, one who has not yet had this experience does not have full consecration or full power for service; hence without Spirit-baptism one's Christian life is incomplete and one's ministry is hampered.

Certain conditions are usually laid down for obtaining

this baptism with the Spirit. Charles W. Conn, a Church of God author, mentions the following: separation from sin, repentance and baptism, the hearing of faith, obedience, intense desire, prayer for the gift.[18] Ralph M. Riggs suggests the following conditions: (1) We must first be saved; (2) we must obey — that is, we must be perfectly surrendered to God; (3) we must ask; (4) we must believe.[19] In this connection Riggs says that it is proper to wait or tarry before the Lord to receive this blessing.[20] Hence Pentecostals often conduct what they call "tarrying meetings" at which people tarry to receive the baptism with the Spirit.

The basic question we must face here is the exegetical one: Does the New Testament teach what our Pentecostal brothers say it does? Is baptism with the Holy Spirit an experience distinct from and subsequent to regeneration — an experience that every believer ought to undergo, the initial physical evidence of which is speaking with tongues?

Let us first see what the New Testament teaches about being baptized in or with the Holy Spirit. There are four instances in the Gospels where John the Baptist is reported as saying that Jesus will baptize with the Holy Spirit: Matthew 3:11, Mark 1:8, Luke 3:16, and John 1:33. The first three of these are parallel passages; the Luke passage (3:16) reads as follows: "I indeed baptize you with water; but one mightier than I cometh, the latchet of whose shoes I am not worthy to unloose; he shall baptize you with the Holy Ghost and with fire." The obvious reference here is to the outpouring of the Spirit which is to come on the Day of Pentecost. John 1:33 reads: "He that sent me to baptize with water, the

18 *Pillars of Pentecost,* pp. 97-105.
19 *Op. cit.,* pp. 102-108.
20 *Ibid.,* p. 107.

same said unto me, Upon whom thou shalt see the Spirit descending, and remaining on him, the same is he which baptizeth with the Holy Ghost." Here again the reference is to the coming outpouring of the Holy Spirit on Pentecost Day.

These words of John the Baptist are quoted by Luke in Acts 1:5 as having been spoken by Jesus: "For John truly baptized with water; but ye shall be baptized with the Holy Ghost not many days hence." Here again the obvious reference is to the outpouring of the Spirit on Pentecost Day. In the second chapter of Acts Luke describes this outpouring, and reports Peter as saying about Christ, "Therefore being by the right hand of God exalted, and having received of the Father the promise of the Holy Ghost, he hath shed forth this, which ye now see and hear" (Acts 2:33). The outpouring of the Spirit at Pentecost, then, is the baptism of the Holy Spirit that both John the Baptist and Jesus had predicted. In the passages so far quoted, therefore, the expression "to be baptized with the Holy Ghost" does not refer to an experience that each individual believer must undergo some time after his regeneration, but to a historical event that took place on the Day of Pentecost.

Was this Pentecostal baptism with the Spirit ever repeated? There is one reference to a repetition of this baptism in Acts 11:16. Peter is at Jerusalem, recounting to the brethren in Judea what had happened to him at the house of Cornelius in Caesarea a few·days before. As I began to speak to Cornelius, Peter says, the Holy Spirit fell on Cornelius and those with him, even as on us at the beginning. And now follows verse 16: "Then remembered I the word of the Lord, how that he said, John indeed baptized with water; but ye shall be baptized with the Holy Ghost." We shall have to grant that this was indeed a repetition of the baptism with the Spirit that occurred on Pentecost. At the time when Cornelius and his kinsmen and friends received this baptism, they spoke with tongues and magnified God (Acts 10:46). We shall have to inquire further into the meaning of this baptism with the Spirit before we can determine whether every believer is expected to go through a similar experience today. It ought to be noted, however, that one cannot use the story of Cornelius to prove that believers must have a Spirit-baptism subsequent to the regeneration that issues in faith, since in this instance faith and baptism with the Spirit occurred simultaneously.

There is one other place in the New Testament where the word *baptize* is associated with the Holy Spirit: I Corinthians 12:13. The truth here under discussion is that of the oneness of the church. The chapter deals with spiritual gifts, but already in verse 4 Paul makes the point that, though there are diversities of gifts, there is only one Spirit who distributes these gifts. In verse 12 Paul uses the analogy of the human body: "For as the body is one, and hath many members, and all the members of that one body, being many, are one body: so also is Christ." Now follows verse 13:

> For by one Spirit are [were, ASV] we all baptized into one body, whether we be Jews or Gentiles, whether we be bond or free; and have been all made to drink into one Spirit.

Some commentators (Calvin, Lenski, Grosheide in the Eerdmans *New International Commentary*) understand *baptized* here as referring to literal water baptism; others (Hodge, Barnes) think of regeneration, which is then figuratively called a baptism in the Spirit. All these writers, however, agree that the passage does not refer to a specific Spirit-baptism distinct from and subsequent to regeneration, but pictures the oneness in Christ that all believers enjoy by virtue of the Spirit's work in regeneration.

Pentecostals agree that the first part of this passage refers to the original salvation experience of the believers here addressed.[21] Riggs claims, however, that the second clause of the verse, "and have been all made to drink into one Spirit" or "of one Spirit" (ASV), refers to the baptism of the Holy Spirit in the Pentecostal sense; he therefore contends that this passage speaks of two experiences: salvation and Spirit-baptism.[22] The second clause, however, is clearly parallel to the first, both clauses stressing the oneness of all believers, and both clauses using the word *all* to indicate that what is said here applies to all believers. If the second clause were to exclude certain believers, Paul's argumentation here would be defeated, since then not all believers would be members of one body. And to suggest, as Riggs does, that all the members of the Corinthian Church had also been Spirit-baptized in the Pentecostal sense[23] flies in the face of Paul's designation of the Corinthians as carnal and as babes in Christ (chapter 3:1). Further, on the premise that this twelfth chapter applies not just to the Corinthians but to all believers,[24] the verse would then teach that all regenerated Christians are also Spirit-baptized in the Pentecostal sense — which teaching Pentecostals reject. We must conclude, therefore, that I Corinthians 12:13 uses the expression "by one Spirit are we all baptized into one body" as a description of the regeneration of all believers that is symbolized by water baptism, and does not picture a "second work of grace"

[21] Riggs, *op. cit.*, pp. 43-44.
[22] *Ibid.*, pp. 58-59.
[23] *Ibid.*, p. 59.
[24] This Pentecostals grant; see Brumback, *op. cit.*, pp. 69-70.

or a "second infilling with the Spirit" or a "second blessing" subsequent to and distinct from regeneration.[25]

These are the only places in the New Testament which speak of a baptism with the Spirit. Pentecostals say, however, that other passages speak of this Spirit-baptism under different terms. It is said, for example, that the expression "sealed with the Spirit" describes the baptism with the Holy Spirit.[26] Passages like II Corinthians 1:22, Ephesians 1:13, and Ephesians 4:30 are said to describe the Spirit-baptism.[27] Let us look at one of these passages, and see how Pentecostals appeal to it: Ephesians 1:13, which reads as follows,

> In whom [in Christ] ye also trusted, after that ye heard the word of truth, the gospel of your salvation: in whom also after that ye believed, ye were sealed with that holy Spirit of promise.

Ralph M. Riggs contends that in this passage "sealed with that Holy Spirit of promise" stands for the baptism with the Holy Spirit.[28] Ernest S. Williams, another Assemblies of God writer, takes the same position.[29] Spirit-baptism, according to the Pentecostal interpretation, is an experience distinct from and subsequent to the new birth, an experience in which one is completely filled with the Holy Spirit. On the basis of the Pentecostal exegesis of Ephesians 1:13, Paul is speaking here about an experience

[25] Note: Some Pentecostals use the expression, "second work of grace," to designate this Spirit-baptism. Others prefer not to use this expression.

[26] From now on I shall use the expression "spirit-baptism" or "baptism with the Holy Spirit" as designating the Pentecostal understanding of this experience (unless otherwise qualified).

[27] Riggs, *op. cit.,* pp. 73-74.

[28] *Ibid.,* pp. 73, 61.

[29] *Op. cit.,* III, 46.

that not all but only some believers enjoy, which is sub-sequent to regeneration.

This, however, cannot be Paul's meaning, since he is clearly speaking here about a blessing that comes to all believers. The entire doxology of verses 3-14 offers praise to God for blessings bestowed on all believers. Paul begins by referring to all the recipients of this letter together with himself when he says, "Blessed be the God and Father of our Lord Jesus Christ, who hath blessed us with all spiritual blessings in heavenly places in Christ" (v. 3). He continues to praise God for these spiritual blessings in succeeding verses. In verse 13 he changes from the first person to the second person: "In whom *ye* also trusted," referring now to his readers apart from himself — not, however, to only some of them but to all of them. "In whom also after that ye believed, ye were sealed with that holy Spirit of promise" is therefore spoken to all the believers addressed. To suggest that a specific group of believers, distinct from the rest, is here intended — people who have had an experience not shared by other believers — is to do violence to the context.

The "sealing with the Spirit" here spoken of refers to the possession of the Spirit as an "earnest" (v. 14) or pledge of the inheritance of eternal life which is ours by faith. The Spirit who dwells in us now seals that inheritance for us, authenticates it, makes us certain of it. But this authentication is not just a blessing shared by a few believers; it is shared by all who truly believe in Christ. For confirmation of this point, note another verse from this epistle, 4:30: "And grieve not the holy Spirit of God, whereby ye are sealed unto the day of redemption." In the earlier verses of this fourth chapter Paul has been addressing all his readers; are we permitted now to assume that in verse 30 he suddenly restricts himself to a select group among them?[30]

Our Pentecostal brothers also contend that the expression "filled with the Spirit" or "filled with the Holy Ghost" describes a postconversion Spirit-baptism.[31] It is true, of course, that the descent of the Spirit on the disciples on the Day of Pentecost is described in Acts 2:4 in these words: "And they were all filled with the Holy Ghost." However, it is said of the company of believers in Acts 4:31, "And when they had prayed, the place was shaken where they were assembled together; and they were all filled with the Holy Ghost. . . ." Many of those here mentioned must have been in the group that received the Spirit on Pentecost Day. If "filled with the Spirit" is understood to mean a postconversion Spirit-baptism, Acts 4:31 makes no sense; many of these disciples had received their baptism with the Spirit (as even Pentecostals would admit),[32] and did not need to receive this again. If the expression "filled with the Spirit" is meant to designate a fresh filling with the Spirit, as I believe,[33] then the passage

[30] The question may be raised whether the reading found in the KJV, "in whom also after that ye believed, ye were sealed . . .", is the best rendering of the Greek. We have here an aorist participle, *pisteusantes,* preceding an aorist finite verb, *esphragisthēte.* One New Testament scholar contends that *pisteusantes* here is a "coincident aorist participle," denoting time coinciding with that of the main verb (E. K. Simpson, *Ephesians* [Grand Rapids: Eerdmans, 1957], p. 35, n. 23, though here the footnote may be by F. F. Bruce). The ASV, in fact, translates, "in whom, having also believed, ye were sealed. . . ." Grammatically, however, the KJ translation is a possible one, since the participle may denote time previous to that of the main verb. The ASV rendering appears preferable, but the argumentation given above does not stand or fall with one translation or the other.

[31] Riggs, *op. cit.,* pp. 69-70.

[32] Brumback, *op. cit.,* pp. 193-94; Riggs, *op. cit.,* p. 118.

[33] Cf. Calvin, Lenski, and F. F. Bruce (in Eerdmans *New International Commentary*), *ad loc.*

says nothing about the teaching under discussion. One is justified, in other words, in drawing from Acts 4:31 the truth that believers need to be filled with the Spirit again and again; one is not justified, however, in drawing from this passage the doctrine that after one has been converted one needs to be baptized with the Spirit as a kind of second blessing.

Pentecostals also point to Ephesians 5:18 as a passage which commands believers to seek the baptism with the Spirit: "And be not drunk with wine, wherein is excess; but be filled with the Spirit."[34] It is certainly true that believers are here commanded to be filled with the Spirit — this no Christian will deny. But the question is: is this filling with the Spirit to be a specific second-blessing experience subsequent to conversion? A careful study of Ephesians 5:18 will reveal that Paul is not talking about a "second-blessing Spirit-baptism" in this passage. In the midst of a very practical series of exhortations he says, "Stop being intoxicated with wine, but be continually filled with the Spirit." Both imperatives here are in the present tense. The prohibition in the present tense ("be not drunk with wine") means "stop doing what you are doing"; the exhortation in the present tense ("be filled with the Spirit") means "do this continually," or "keep on doing this." What Paul is enjoining here, in other words, is a continuing state of being filled with the Spirit, not a single, once-for-all second-blessing experience. Far from implying that his readers have not received the Spirit, he assumes that they have been sealed with the Spirit (1:13), and he now urges them to be always filled with that Spirit who has given them new life in Christ. Ephesians 5:18, therefore, does

[34] Riggs, *op. cit.,* pp. 83, 103.

not teach that believers must seek a baptism with the Holy Spirit as a once-for-all second-blessing experience.[35]

The only clear instance, therefore, in which the New Testament speaks of a baptism with the Spirit as occurring subsequent to Pentecost is the case of Cornelius. We should immediately add, however, that there are two other instances where we read of a receiving of the Holy Spirit as a kind of public experience after Pentecost: in Acts 8, where speaking with tongues is not specifically mentioned, and in Acts 19, where speaking with tongues and prophesying are mentioned. Pentecostals claim that these three instances — the Samaritans in Acts 8, Cornelius in Acts 10 and 11, and the Ephesian believers in Acts 19 — when taken together with the Pentecost narrative of Acts 2, constitute clear Scriptural evidence for the necessity of a postconversion Spirit-baptism. The Pentecostal case for Spirit-baptism, in fact, stands or falls with the Acts material, for Brumback admits that "in I Corinthians 12-14 there is not the slightest hint that the gift of tongues is associated, in any direct sense, with the filling with the Holy Spirit. . . ."[36] If this is so, one cannot prove from the Corinthians material that glossolalia is the initial physical evidence of the baptism with the Spirit; one will have to prove this from the book of Acts. Accordingly, we shall now take a closer look at the above-named passages from Acts.

On the day of Pentecost the disciples "were all filled with the Holy Ghost, and began to speak with other tongues, as the Spirit gave them utterance" (Acts 2:4). Why was the gift of tongues given to the 120 disciples at

[35] It is difficult to see how Pentecostals can justifiably claim that two expressions occurring in the same epistle, "sealed with the Spirit" (1:13) and "be filled with the Spirit" (5:18) both designate Spirit-baptism. For why should Paul in 5:18 urge his readers to seek what according to 1:13 they already have?

[36] *Op. cit.*, p. 266.

this time? At least two reasons may be given: (1) Their ability to speak with tongues was a sign that they had truly received the promised fulness of the Spirit — this sign was given, it will be recalled, along with two other signs: the sound as of a rushing mighty wind, and the tongues as of fire which sat upon each of them. (2) Their ability to speak with tongues was to give them assurance that the Holy Spirit would enable them to communicate the truths of the gospel to all the world. I am not suggesting that the disciples actually used tongues in witnessing to foreigners, for we have no evidence that they did (even on the Day of Pentecost Peter apparently preached in Aramaic, the common spoken language of Palestine), but I am saying that the glossolalia in which they engaged served as an encouraging sign that the Spirit would give them power to witness to all the nations of the world.

What the 120 received on Pentecost Day, therefore, were three miraculous signs to assure them that the promised outpouring of the Spirit had really occurred. Tongue-speaking was only one of these signs. When Pentecostals contend that the experience of the disciples at Pentecost is the pattern for all believers today,[37] why do they think only of glossolalia and not of the sound of the wind and the fiery tongues?

At this time Peter said to the multitude, "Repent, and be baptized every one of you in the name of Jesus Christ for the remission of sins, and ye shall receive the gift of the Holy Ghost" (Acts 2:38). Pentecostals claim that "the gift of the Holy Spirit," as here described, means Spirit-baptism accompanied by tongues.[38] This is, of course, a possible interpretation. It does not seem likely, however, for two reasons: (1) Though we do read that many wonders

37 Brumback, *op. cit.,* pp. 196ff.
38 *Ibid.,* pp. 238-40; Riggs, *op. cit.,* p. 118.

and signs were done through the apostles (v. 43), we do not read that the three thousand who were converted on the Day of Pentecost spoke with tongues; and (2) when thus interpreted, the passage proves too much even for Pentecostals, since Peter would be implying that the repentance which brings one into possession of the remission of sins is sufficient for the reception of Spirit-baptism — in other words, that all believers automatically receive Spirit-baptism followed by tongues. I prefer to believe, with Calvin, Lenski, and Bruce, that "the gift of the Holy Spirit" here means the Holy Spirit Himself as He imparts the blessings of salvation, with no specific reference to charismatic gifts such as glossolalia. When thus understood, Acts 2 does not prove that every believer must receive a Spirit-baptism some time after he has come to faith. Peter's injunction to the multitude, in fact, rather implies that it is when one repents and believes that he receives the Holy Spirit, not at some later time.

Do the other incidents reported in Acts which speak of the receiving of the Spirit prove the point at issue? Let us look next at Acts 8:4-24. Philip had gone down to the city of Samaria to proclaim Christ to the Samaritans — a mixed race, partly Jewish, partly Gentile. Since the Samaritans had broken away from the Jewish faith, their religion was a mixture of truth and falsehood. Since they were a mixed race, and since they had tried to sabotage the rebuilding of Jerusalem's temple and walls (Ezra 4: 4, 5), the Jews hated the Samaritans and "had no dealings" with them (John 4:9). These facts made the revival in Samaria all the more significant.

Philip not only preached but also performed miracles: he cast out unclean spirits and healed paralytics. The result of his work was that many believed and were baptized. Later two of the apostles, Peter and John, were sent to

Samaria. They "prayed for them [the Samaritans], that they might receive the Holy Ghost: (for as yet he was fallen upon none of them. . . .) Then laid they their hands on them, and they received the Holy Ghost" (Acts 8:15-17). Note that it was through the agency of the apostles that this reception of the Holy Spirit occurred.

At first glance, this passage looks like strong proof for the Pentecostal position. Here were people who were believers but apparently did not at first receive the fullness of the Spirit. When the apostles had laid their hands on them, they did receive the Holy Spirit. Hence, so Pentecostals conclude, believers today must receive the baptism of the Spirit in a distinct experience subsequent to their having come to faith.[39]

What actually happened at Samaria? Previous to the coming of Peter and John, Philip had wrought many miracles. After the Samaritan believers had received the Spirit, Simon the Sorcerer wanted to buy the power of bestowing the Holy Spirit. Though we are not told in so many words that the Samaritans spoke with tongues after the apostles had laid their hands upon them, it is obvious that there must have been some public evidence of their having received the Spirit. We may therefore agree with our Pentecostal friends at this point that the Samaritans probably did speak with tongues — though it should be remembered that Luke does not say that they did. It may also be that the Samaritans revealed the presence of other charismatic gifts: prophecy, perhaps, or gifts of healing. The latter gift had been exercised previously by Philip; if it were later exercised by a number of Samaritans, this would make quite an impression on Simon, who had earlier been amazing people with his magical powers.

But now the question arises: why were these special gifts

39 Brumback, *op. cit.*, pp. 205-214; Riggs, *op. cit.*, pp. 51-53, 109.

of the Spirit bestowed on the Samaritans? One answer, and an important one, would be to say that here in Samaria the power of the gospel was thus conquering the occult power of magical arts. This would be important because of the local situation. But an even more important reason would be this: the Samaritan church was thus placed on full equality with the Jerusalem church, since to the Samaritans also were given the special gifts of the Spirit. Thus the Jewish Christians, who tended to look down on the Samaritans, would be assured that the Samaritans had equal rights in the church with themselves. We could thus call what happened in Samaria a kind of extension of Pentecost, made necessary because the Church was now expanding into what was previously hostile territory. Given the Jewish prejudice against the Samaritans, it can well be imagined that it would take a tremendous demonstration of the power of the Spirit to convince die-hards among the Jewish Christians that it was really proper to bring the gospel to the Samaritans.

Does this passage prove that every believer must receive a Spirit-baptism subsequent to conversion? As we shall see a little later, many cases are reported in the book of Acts where these special gifts of the Spirit were apparently not bestowed on people after they came to faith. Obviously, therefore, what happened at Samaria was something exceptional. This being so, we have no right to conclude that every believer must receive special gifts of the Spirit comparable to those bestowed at Samaria.

We turn next to Acts 10:44-46, the passage which describes the falling of the Spirit upon Cornelius and those who were with him. While Peter was speaking at the house of Cornelius, so we read here, the Holy Spirit fell on all them that heard the word; and the Jews who were with Peter (later described as being six in number) were amazed, for they heard these Gentiles speaking with tongues and magnifying God. In Chapter 11:15-17 we find Peter rehearsing these events before the brethren in Jerusalem; it will be recalled that here he describes what had happened as a baptism with or in the Holy Spirit. Peter here also draws a comparison between what had happened at Caesarea and what had occurred on Pentecost Day: "Forasmuch then as God gave them the like gift as he did unto us, who believed on the Lord Jesus Christ; what was I, that I could withstand God?" (verse 17). In other words, Peter adduces the bestowal of the Spirit in a special way upon Cornelius and his group as indisputable evidence that God was accepting Gentiles into His covenant.

Does this passage support the Pentecostal contention that every believer must have a Spirit-baptism subsequent to conversion?[40] No, it does not; we have already noted that in Cornelius' case the bestowal of the Spirit was simultaneous with his coming to faith. Further, we should again observe that the bestowal upon Cornelius and his group of certain special gifts of the Spirit (they spoke with tongues and magnified God, 10:46) served a unique purpose. For centuries Jews had not brought God's saving truth to Gentiles, except in rare instances. Peter himself had had so many objections to going to Cornelius' house that he had to have a special vision and a special voice from heaven to persuade him to go. It would take a mighty demonstration of the power of the Spirit to persuade the ultra-conservative Jewish Christians in Jerusalem that from now on Gentiles were to have equal opportunities to receive the gospel along with Jews. If anything, the barrier between Jews and Gentiles was even greater than that between Jews and Samaritans!

[40] See Brumback, *op. cit.,* pp. 219-222; Riggs, *op. cit.,* pp. 87-88; Nelson, *op. cit.,* pp. 95-96.

So now we see the reason for the bestowal of the special gifts of the Spirit upon Cornelius and his household. This bestowal was a clear demonstration that Gentiles could be saved and that the Jewish Christians did not need to hesitate to receive converted Gentiles into their fellowship. What happened at Caesarea was therefore another extension of Pentecost, this time into the circle of the Gentiles. That this was an extension or repetition of Pentecost is quite clear from Acts 11:15, where Luke records Peter as saying, "And as I began to speak, the Holy Ghost fell on them, as on us at the beginning," and from verse 17, where Peter goes on to say, "Forasmuch . . . as God gave them the like gift as he did unto us." The reception of the charismatic gifts of the Spirit placed these Gentiles on equality with the Christian Samaritans and the Christian Jews. But not all who came to faith in those days are said to have received these charismatic gifts, as we shall see a little later. Hence the fact that Cornelius and his household received the ability to speak with tongues by no means proves that every believer should receive this gift.

We turn now to Acts 19:1-7, probably the most baffling of all the passages in Acts associated with glossolalia. When Paul came to Ephesus on his third missionary journey, he found there certain disciples, twelve in number. The question which he first asked them is often quoted as in the King James Version: "Have ye received the Holy Ghost since ye believed?" (verse 2). When the question is read in this way,[41] it seems to support the Pentecostal contention that one must receive the Holy Spirit some time

---

41 It is so quoted by Nelson, *op. cit.*, p. 96. Riggs, though quoting the passage in this way, adds after *since* the words *or when* in parentheses, indicating that he recognizes the questionableness of the King James rendering (*op. cit.*, p. 61).

after one has become a believer. It may well be questioned, however, whether the King James rendering is here to be preferred. The Greek has *ei pneuma hagion elabete pisteusantes*. We have here a finite verb in the aorist tense (*elabete*), followed by an aorist participle (*pisteusantes*). It will, of course, be granted that the tense of the participle in Greek does not convey any idea of time, and that an aorist participle can therefore express time either contemporaneous with the main verb or before that of the main verb. The determination of the time of the participle is dependent on the context.

In the abstract, therefore, the King James rendering is a possible one. The question is, however, whether the context demands it. Actually, the context is not decisive here, since these disciples had not received the Holy Spirit up to the time the question was asked. It is generally assumed by interpreters of the passage that "receiving the Holy Spirit" here refers specifically to the reception of the special charismatic manifestations of the Spirit, such as tongue-speaking. If we now try to settle the question by looking at precedents, we still fail to get a decisive answer, since at Samaria the charismatic gifts were bestowed after the first exercise of faith, whereas at Caesarea these gifts were bestowed simultaneously with faith.

If the intention had been to make a real issue of the priority of faith to the reception of the Spirit, Luke could certainly have added some words or changed the construction of the sentence to make this plain. The most natural reading of the question in verse 2 is certainly this: "Did you receive the Holy Spirit when you believed?" (literally, *did you receive the Holy Spirit believing?*). Though the interpretation of the entire passage does not depend on the translation of this verse, therefore, and though I would grant that the King James rendering is a possible one, I believe the rendering of the ASV is here to be preferred: "Did ye receive the Holy Spirit when ye believed?"[42]

The answer of the twelve disciples is quite revealing: "Nay, we did not so much as hear whether the Holy Spirit was given" (ASV). The Greek text literally reads, "We have never even heard that there is a Holy Spirit." However, we have a similar construction in John 7:39, where the best attested Greek text has, "For the Spirit was not yet, because Jesus was not yet glorified"; here the translators have rendered the verse: "For the Spirit (or Holy Ghost) was not yet given." So in Acts 19:2 the word *given* should be added in the translation, as the ASV does.[43] What their answer means is this: these Ephesian believers "had not yet heard about the giving or outpouring of the Spirit —in other words, they were ignorant regarding the event of Pentecost."[44]

Paul next found out that they had been baptized into John's baptism. It may very well be that they had been baptized by Apollos, who had come to Ephesus previous to Paul's arrival, and who knew only the baptism of John (Acts 18:25). The baptism of John was a pre-Pentecostal baptism. Paul now explained to these believers that since Christ had come, had accomplished His mission on earth, had been raised from the dead, and had poured out the Holy Spirit upon the church, this anticipatory baptism was

[42] Both the Revised Standard Version and the New English Bible have basically this translation of verse 2. Most commentators also prefer the ASV rendering: e.g., Lenski, Alford, R. J. Knowling (in *The Expositor's Greek Testament*), Grosheide (in *Korte Verklaring*). F. F. Bruce insists that the rendering "when ye believed" is "doctrinally important," quoting J. H. Moulton's *Grammar of N.T. Greek* (*Acts*, in *New International Commentary*, p. 385, n. 8).

[43] Cf. F. F. Bruce, *op. cit.*, p. 385.

[44] B. Van Elderen, "Glossolalia in the New Testament," *Bulletin of the Evangelical Theological Society*, VII, 2 (Spring, 1964), p. 55.

inappropriate.[45] Accordingly, Paul now baptized them into the name of the Lord Jesus — this was not really a rebaptism, but their first Christian baptism, necessary because they had only been baptized with John's baptism. After he had baptized them, Paul laid his hands upon them, and "the Holy Ghost came on them; and they spake with tongues, and prophesied" (Acts 19:6).

Why, now, did these twelve disciples at Ephesus receive the gift of tongues and the gift of prophecy — two of the special gifts of the Holy Spirit? Because they had not even heard about the outpouring of the Holy Spirit, and therefore had to be convinced beyond the shadow of a doubt that this great redemptive fact had indeed occurred. Though Paul had probably told them about Pentecost, and had described the special signs given to the disciples on that day, the surest way of convincing these Ephesians that Pentecost had occurred was to give them two of the special gifts of the Spirit which had been bestowed on the disciples on that day: glossolalia and prophecy. In other words, here was a kind of extension of Pentecost to Ephesus, necessary because a prominent group of believers there (Bruce calls them the nucleus of the Ephesian church) [46] had an understanding of Christianity which was wholly inadequate. Whereas glossolalia at Samaria and Caesarea had occurred primarily for the sake of the church at large, glossolalia at Ephesus occurred primarily for the sake of these Ephesian believers, and for the sake of the Ephesian church of which they were to form the nucleus. It will be remembered that it was at Ephesus that Aquila and Priscilla had to expound to Apollos the way of God more accurately, and that Apollos had been very influential in this city. In other words, there may have

45 Bruce, *op. cit.*, p. 386.
46 *Ibid.*, p. 387.

been others at Ephesus who had been baptized only with the baptism of John, and who therefore also needed incontrovertible proof that the Holy Spirit had indeed been poured out on Pentecost Day.

Going back now to our main question, does what happened at Ephesus prove that every believer must receive a tongues-attested Spirit-baptism subsequent to his conversion? It does not, for two reasons: (1) The faith which these Ephesian believers had when Paul first came to them was not full-orbed Christian faith but a faith which was quite incomplete. (2) There were special circumstances which made the bestowal of glossolalia on these Ephesian disciples necessary; hence we are not justified in concluding that the reception of the gift of tongues by these disciples constituted a normative pattern for all believers.

Three observations are now in order about the bestowals of the special gifts of the Spirit on the groups just described:

(1) In each of the above four instances (Pentecost, Samaria, Caesarea, and Ephesus), the special gifts of the Spirit, including tongue-speaking (if we assume that tongue-speaking occurred among the Samaritans), were bestowed on entire groups. In none of these cases do we find what is commonly found in Pentecostal churches: namely, that some in the congregation have received the baptism of the Spirit and have therefore exercised glossolalia, whereas others have not done so.

(2) In the last three of the instances we have just examined, the special gifts of the Spirit (including particularly the ability to speak with tongues) were bestowed upon people who did not ask for them. This was true at Samaria (the apostles prayed that the Samaritans might receive the Holy Spirit, but we are not told that the Samaritans did), at Caesarea (where the falling of the Spirit on Cornelius' household was as much of a surprise to Cornelius as it was

to Peter), and at Ephesus (where Paul did lay his hands on the Ephesian believers, but where we are not told that the Ephesians themselves asked for a special bestowal of the Spirit upon them). When Pentecostals suggest that the baptism in the Holy Spirit, which is to be followed by tongue-speaking, must be wrested from the Lord by believers through agonizing prayer, they are setting up a requirement which was not demanded in the case of the Samaritans, the household of Cornelius, or the disciples at Ephesus.

(3) Though it is true that the 120 disciples did tarry at Jerusalem while waiting for the outpouring of the Holy Spirit, since Jesus had instructed them to do so (Luke 24: 49), we do not read that any of the other three groups were engaged in a similar kind of "tarrying for the Holy Spirit." The Samaritan converts were not doing this before Peter and John came, and neither were the disciples at Ephesus before Paul came. As for Cornelius, though he was waiting for Peter to come to him, since he had been instructed in a vision to send for Peter (10:5), he was not particularly tarrying for the baptism of the Holy Spirit, but was waiting for the message of the gospel to be brought to him. When, therefore, Pentecostals urge people to take part in "tarrying meetings" — meetings often lasting long into the night, at which people wait to receive the baptism with the Holy Spirit — appealing to Luke 24:49 for support,[47] they are making an improper application of this passage. The passage reads: "And, behold, I send the promise of my Father upon you: but tarry ye in the city of

---

[47] Riggs, *op. cit.*, pp. 106-107. Though Riggs does not mention "tarrying meetings," he does say that "tarrying before the Lord is always Scriptural and is normal procedure in receiving from God," tying this in with the experience of the disciples before Pentecost. By "receiving from God" he means receiving Spirit-baptism. Cf. also Nelson, *op. cit.*, pp. 98-99.

Jerusalem, until ye be endued with power from on high."
Jesus gave His disciples these instructions in connection
with a specific historical event that was about to occur:
the outpouring of the Holy Spirit. To make "tarrying
meetings" part of the regular program of the church is to
make a normative practice out of something which was
commanded at a specific time in history in preparation for
a unique event.

Before taking leave of this Acts material, I should like to
point out that aside from the four incidents just described,
there is no mention of glossolalia in the book of Acts. When
Pentecostals tells us that they are convinced of the importance of tongue-speaking because of its frequent occur-
rence in the book of Acts, they are reading far more tongue-
speaking into Acts than the facts warrant. We noted earlier
that, according to Pentecostals, the expression "filled with
the Spirit" designates a postconversion Spirit-baptism, which
is attested by glossolalia.[48] I have found, however, the following instances in the book of Acts where people are
described as being filled with the Spirit or full of the Holy
Spirit, and where no mention whatever is made of tongue-
speaking: Acts 4:8 (Peter before the Sanhedrin), 4:31
(the believers praying together — this passage I discussed
before), 6:3 (the seven deacons), 6:5 and 7:55 (Stephen),
9:17 (Saul at the time of his baptism),[49] 11:24 (Barnabas),
13:9 (Paul on Cyprus), 13:52 (the disciples at Antioch of
Pisidia). Only once in Acts is the expression "filled with

[48] Riggs, *op. cit.,* pp. 69-70.

[49] Pentecostals assume that at this time Saul began to speak with
tongues, since he later claimed to speak with tongues more than the
Corinthians (I Cor. 14:18), and since he must have started speaking
with tongues at some time (Brumback, *op. cit.,* pp. 215-17; Nelson,
op. cit., p. 97). That the Apostle Paul spoke with tongues is clearly
attested by Scripture. That he began to speak with tongues when
he was baptized, however, is an assumption for which there is no
Scriptural proof.

the Holy Spirit" applied to people who received the gift of tongues: Acts 2:4. This expression is not used in connection with the Samaritans, the household of Cornelius, or the Ephesian believers. In the other nine instances where the expression "filled with the Spirit" is used in Acts, tongue-speaking is not mentioned. Pentecostals, therefore, are not justified in assuming that this expression always describes a Spirit-baptism followed by glossolalia.

But there is more evidence against the Pentecostal position. Repeatedly we are told by Pentecostals that the pattern of the book of Acts is normative for Christians today. It is then simply assumed that the cases where people are said to have spoken with tongues set the pattern for today. There were, however, as we have seen, exceptional reasons why glossolalia was bestowed at Pentecost, Samaria, Caesarea, and Ephesus — reasons that do not apply to all believers today. To prove this latter point, I now adduce the following instances recorded in the book of Acts of people who were brought to salvation but are not said to have spoken with tongues: 2:41 (the 3,000 converted on Pentecost Day), 3:7-9 (the lame man who was healed), 4:4 (those converted after the healing of the lame man, when the number of the men came to be about 5,000), 5:14 (the many who became believers after the death of Ananias and Sapphira), 6:7 (a great company of priests), 8:36 (the Ethiopian eunuch), 9:42 (the many who believed after Dorcas was raised), 11:21 (those who turned to the Lord in Syrian Antioch), 13:12 (the proconsul at Cyprus), 13:43 and 48 (believers in Pisidian Antioch), 14:1 (believers in Iconium), 14:21 (disciples at Derbe), 16:14 (Lydia), 16:34 (the Philippian jailor), 17:4 (the believers in Thessalonica), 17:11-12 (the Bereans), 17:34 (the Athenians), 18:4 (those at Corinth), 18:8 (Crispus and other Corinthians), 28:24 (some of the Jews at Rome). It should now be clear that the evidence found in the book of Acts does not bear out the Pentecostal contention that glossolalia following upon an experience of Spirit-baptism is the normal New Testament pattern for all believers.

Summarizing, we have found that the expression "baptize with the Spirit" is used four times in the Gospels and once in Acts to designate the historic event of the outpouring of the Spirit on the Day of Pentecost. Only once is the expression used to point to a repetition of this baptism — in Acts 11:16, where it refers to what happened at Caesarea. What happened at Caesarea was an extension of Pentecost to the Gentiles, just as what happened at Samaria was an extension of Pentecost to the Samaritans, and as what happened at Ephesus was an extension of Pentecost to disciples who had not even heard that the Holy Spirit had been poured out. In each case there were special circumstances which made this kind of extension necessary. By far the majority of those whom the author of Acts reports as coming to the faith, however, are not said to have spoken with tongues. There is, further, no proof that such expressions as "sealed with the Spirit" or "filled with the Spirit" point to a postconversion Spirit-baptism attested by tongue-speaking. I conclude, therefore, that there is no Biblical evidence for the Pentecostal doctrine that every believer should seek a postconversion Spirit-baptism which is to be evidenced by the initial physical sign of glossolalia.

4. *The discussion of tongue-speaking in I Corinthians 12-14.*

These chapters constitute the only section of the Bible where glossolalia is discussed in detail; hence it is important that we know their main teaching. It may be observed at the outset that if glossolalia is as important as Pentecostals and Neo-Pentecostals say it is, it is strange indeed that Paul discusses tongue-speaking in only one of his epistles, and that no reference to the subject is found in any other New Testament epistle. This is not to suggest that the treatment of glossolalia in I Corinthians 12-14 is not important, but only to say that tongue-speaking plays a relatively minor role in the New Testament.

Before proceeding to analyze the teaching of these chapters, however, we should face one or two prior questions. Were the tongues spoken at Corinth similar to the glossolalia reported in the book of Acts? Most Pentecostals, as we have seen, seem to take the position that, as regards their nature, the tongues spoken at Corinth and those spoken at Pentecost were identical, but that they differed in the purposes for which they were used.

As we compare the accounts in Acts with the discussion in I Corinthians, it becomes clear that there were significant differences between the glossolalia reported in Acts and that which took place in Corinth: (1) Glossolalia at Corinth could only be understood when it was interpreted; this, however, does not appear to have been true in the cases of tongue-speaking reported in Acts. (2) The purpose of glossolalia in Corinth was edification, either for the individual himself or for the congregation (in case the tongues were interpreted). The purpose of glossolalia in Acts, however, was validation and confirmation of the outpouring of the Holy Spirit. (3) The glossolalia reported in Acts occurred under very special circumstances, when an extension of Pentecost was necessary. There is no indication, however, that such special circumstances were present in Corinth. (4) In Acts glossolalia "appears to have been an irresistible and temporary initial experience, but at Corinth it was a continuing gift under the control of the speaker (I Cor. 14:27, 28)."[50] (5) In each instance of glossolalia reported in Acts, everyone in the group involved spoke with tongues. In Corinth, however, not all spoke with tongues (see I Corinthians 12:30).

I believe, therefore, that there were important differences between the glossolalia reported in Acts and that reported in I Corinthians. Whether these differences concerned only purpose and operation, but not the nature of the glossolalia itself, as Brumback contends,[51] is hard to say. Commentators are sharply divided on the question; though most of them agree that the tongues on the Day of Pentecost were foreign languages, some hold that the tongues at Corinth were also foreign languages, while others insist that the tongues at Corinth were ecstatic utterances different from ordinary human languages. It seems difficult, if not impossible, to make a final judgment on this matter. We do know that glossolalia was a spiritual gift bestowed on a number of the members of the Corinthian Church.

I shall return later to the question of whether we are justified in assuming that glossolalia is one of the gifts of the Spirit which is still in the church today. Pentecostals insist that the gift of tongues, as well as the other special, miraculous gifts of the Spirit mentioned in I Corinthians 12:8-10 and 28, is still in the church today. Let us at this juncture give our Pentecostal and Neo-Pentecostal brothers the benefit of the doubt, and let us assume for the time being that glossolalia is one of the gifts which the Holy Spirit still distributes to believers today. Against the background of this assumption, let us see what Paul says about tongue-speaking in I Corinthians 12 to 14.

[50] W. G. Putnam, "Tongues, Gift of," *New Bible Dictionary* (Grand Rapids: Eerdmans, 1962), p. 1286. See also B. Van Elderen, *loc. cit.,* p. 56.

[51] *Op. cit.,* pp. 249-50, 263-64.

We should remind ourselves, however, that Paul's discussion of tongue-speaking in I Corinthians cannot be used to prove that glossolalia is the indispensable evidence of one's having received the baptism with the Holy Spirit. For Carl Brumback himself concedes that glossolalia in I Corinthians has nothing directly to do with being filled with the Spirit.[52] It will be recalled that Pentecostals distinguish between tongues as evidence for Spirit-baptism and tongues as a gift which one may continue to exercise.[53] Our Pentecostal friends contend that the references to tongues found in the book of Acts describe tongues as "evidence," whereas the discussion of tongues in I Corinthians deals with tongues as a "gift."[54] According to their own admission, therefore, one cannot prove from the passages in I Corinthians that tongue-speaking is the evidence for Spirit-baptism. The case for glossolalia as evidence for Spirit-baptism will therefore have to stand or fall on the material in the book of Acts.

What do Pentecostals, then, draw from the Corinthians material? The thought that glossolalia is a valuable spiritual gift. The value of this gift, so they say, is twofold: it has a devotional purpose and a congregational purpose.[55] Insisting that Paul in these chapters does not disparage

[52] "In I Corinthians 12-14 there is not the slightest hint that the gift of tongues is associated, in any direct sense, with the filling with the Holy Spirit, certainly not in any greater degree than the other gifts. Its sole purpose is the personal edification of the speaker, and, when coupled with interpretation, the edification of the hearers" (*ibid.*, p. 266.).

[53] *Statement of Fundamental Truths* (Assemblies of God), Article 8. Cf. Brumback, *op. cit.*, pp. 261-72; Gee, *op. cit.*, p. 91; and Thomas F. Zimmerman, "Plea for Pentecostals," *Christianity Today*, VII (Jan. 4, 1962), p. 12: "Speaking in tongues as the initial evidence should be distinguished . . . from the gift of tongues as described in I Corinthians 12:10."

[54] Brumback, *op. cit.*, p. 262. Cf. note 53, above.

[55] Brumback, *op. cit.*, pp. 291-317.

glossolalia, Brumback answers several arguments for downgrading tongues on the basis of the Corinthians material,[56] and even lists fifteen statements from I Corinthians 14 which, he contends, show that Paul favored the gift of tongues.[57]

We turn, then, to I Corinthians 12-14 to see whether these chapters attach as high a value to glossolalia as do present-day tongue-speakers. We ought, however, first to ask a question or two about the nature of the church at Corinth. The Corinthian Church was a problem church. As someone has said, it gave Paul more headaches and heartaches than any other church he served. Some of the problems he had to deal with there were: the problem of factionalism and contentiousness, the toleration of gross immorality, the conducting of lawsuits against each other, the temptation to fall back into idolatry through eating meats offered to idols, abuses in connection with the Lord's Supper, and the denial of the resurrection of the body.[58]

Against this background we can understand that the Corinthians also had a problem in connection with spiritual gifts. Their problem was not that they were lacking in spiritual gifts (see 1:7, "ye come behind in no gift"), but that they were abusing them. It becomes evident from chapters 12 to 14 that many Corinthians were placing the gift of tongues at the top of the list of spiritual endowments, were priding themselves on possessing it, and were exercising it to excess in meetings of the congregation. The prevalence of a kind of ecstatic speech among the frenzied priests and priestesses of the Greek oracles (particularly that of Apollo at Delphi, which was not far away) would

[56] *Ibid.*, pp. 147-79.

[57] *Ibid.*, p. 168.

[58] See Donald Metz, *Speaking in Tongues,* pp. 78-82, for a detailed analysis of these problems.

help to account for the high value placed on tongue-speaking by the Corinthians.[59] As we now study what Paul wrote about glossolalia in these chapters, it will become quite clear that one of his main purposes was to show that the gift of tongues was not nearly as valuable as many of the Corinthians thought it was.

What strikes us first is that in the two listings of spiritual gifts given in chapter 12 (in vv. 8-10 and 28) tongues and the interpretation of tongues are mentioned last. This position is intentional. Paul's evaluation of the gift of tongues is so different from that of the Corinthians that, though many Corinthians were inclined to place this gift first, he places it last. What is even more striking, in fact, is that in two other lists of spiritual gifts and offices, namely, Ephesians 4:11-12 and Romans 12:6-8, tongues are not mentioned at all! In the Romans passage Paul mentions such gifts as exhorting, giving, ruling, and showing mercy; surely if the gift of tongues were one of the outstanding endowments of the Spirit, it ought to have been specified here — but we find no trace of it. In I Corinthians 12 Paul is therefore saying to the Corinthians: since there are so many gifts of the Spirit, why go to such lengths to stress the very least of these gifts? Surely, too, the order of these listings has a message for contemporary tongue-speakers, who seem to want to exalt the gift of tongues as if it were the spiritual gift *par excellence!*[60]

In verses 12-27 of I Corinthians 12 Paul compares the Church to a body with many members. His point is that various members of the church have various gifts, and that we cannot therefore expect everyone to have the same gift. In verse 17 Paul says, "If the whole body were an eye, where were the hearing?" We might paraphrase this passage to

59 Van Elderen, *loc. cit.*, p. 56.
60 Cf. Metz, *op. cit.*, pp. 85-86.

read as follows: "If the whole body consisted of tongue-speakers, where were the teachers?" And in verse 11 Paul asserts that the gifts all come from the Spirit, who divides to each one severally even as he will. The thrust of Paul's argument is: don't all of you desire the gift of tongues, since you do not know whether the Spirit wants to give all of you this gift, and since the church would not be a very good body if every member of it performed exactly the same function.

From verse 30 of this chapter we learn that not all the members of the Corinthian Church had the gift of tongues: "Do all speak with tongues?" As we read the chapter, we get the impression that those who did not have the gift of tongues were tempted to feel somewhat inferior to those who did, since so much was being made of this gift. The thrust of Paul's discussion in verses 12-27, however, is that a person who does not have the gift of tongues is not one whit inferior to one who does, and that the position in the church of one who does not speak with tongues is not less important than that of one who does speak with tongues. All members of the body of Christ are necessary, and therefore one member may not say to the other, "I have no need of you" (v. 21). The teaching of Scripture here would rule out any claim that the possession of the gift of tongues gives one a position of spiritual pre-eminence over others who do not possess this gift. It may further be observed that Paul would not have said anything like this if it were true, as our Pentecostal brothers claim, that the ability to speak with tongues (even as an initial experience) sets a person off from other believers as one who has received a fullness of the Spirit which others have not received. There is not the slightest hint in this chapter or in chapter 14 that tongue-speaking can have any such significance as

Pentecostals ascribe to it in connection with the baptism of the Holy Spirit.

In 12:31 Paul says, "But covet earnestly the best gifts" (or the *greater* gifts, if we follow the American Standard Version here). His words imply that there are gifts of greater and lesser value. By placing tongues and the interpretation of tongues last in his two listings of spiritual gifts, Paul intimates that he does not consider the gift of tongues to be one of the greater gifts.

"Yet," Paul continues, "shew I unto you a more excellent way" — and now follows the well-known chapter on love (chapter 13). Though this chapter is often read by itself, it has a very important function in the context. Before further discussing the precise value of tongues, Paul wants to tell the Corinthians and us that there is something far more important, not only than the gift of tongues, but than the other special gifts of the Spirit as well. Therefore he says, "If I speak with the tongues of men and of angels, but have not love, I am become sounding brass, or a clanging cymbal" (13:1).[61] Not that anybody claimed to speak with the tongues of angels — the sentence is hypothetical. Suppose, Paul says, that I had reached the very highest peak of tongue-speaking; suppose I were able to speak not only with unknown human tongues but even with the tongues of angels — if I had no love, I would be only a noisy gong or a clanging cymbal. My life would be empty, hollow, and hypocritical.

The lesson is obvious. Though there may be some value in speaking with tongues — a limited value, as we shall see in a moment — it is far more important that our lives should be filled with love. Our primary concern, therefore,

___

[61] I quote here, and in the next three instances, from the ASV, since the word "charity" used in the King James Version no longer conveys to modern readers the intended meaning.

may never be just the cultivation of a gift like tongue-speaking; it must always be the cultivation of love, which is greater even than faith or hope. Though Paul is to place a higher value on prophecy than on tongues in chapter 14, verse two of chapter 13 teaches that the cultivation of love is more important even than the exercise of the gift of prophecy: "If I have the gift of prophecy . . . but have not love, I am nothing." The burden of the entire chapter is: if I "have not love, it profiteth me nothing" (verse 3).

Paul begins chapter 14 by repeating the main thrust of chapter 13: "Follow after love; yet desire earnestly spiritual gifts, but rather that ye may prophesy." In other words, whatever spiritual gifts you have, they must always be used in such a way as to be expressions of love; otherwise you will be abusing them. Any use of a gift for your own prestige or honor is therefore wrong — apparently Paul was here probing a sore spot in the Corinthian Church.

Whereas many Corinthians seem to have preferred the gift of tongues above all others, Paul places the gift of prophecy above that of tongues: "but rather that ye may prophesy." The reason given is really an amplification of chapter 13: ". . . He that prophesieth speaketh unto men to edification, and exhortation, and comfort. He that speaketh in an unknown tongue edifieth himself; but he that prophesieth edifieth the church" (vv. 3,4).[62] Tongues as spoken in Corinth were apparently not understood by the hearers unless they were interpreted. In view of the importance of love and in view of the fact that with our gifts we are to serve the whole church, it is obvious that prophecy is superior to tongues.[63] For, though with tongues we edify

[62] It should be noted that the word *unknown* in v. 4 is in italics, indicating that it has been added by the translators. The original has simply, "in a tongue" (*glōssē*).

[63] The gift of prophecy spoken of in this chapter, as most commentators agree, is probably to be understood as a special charismatic

ourselves (which is good), by means of prophecy we edify the whole church (which is much better). Hence, Paul continues, "I would that ye all spake with tongues, but rather that ye prophesied: for greater is he that prophesieth than he that speaketh with tongues, except he interpret, that the church may receive edifying" (verse 5). It is as if I might say to my seminary students: I would like to have you all play the piano, but I would rather have you preach the Word with power and persuasiveness. Calvin puts it this way:

> He [Paul] observes, therefore, an admirable medium, by disapproving of nothing that was useful, while at the same time he exhorts them not to prefer, by an absurd zeal, things of less consequence to what was of primary importance.[64]

In verses 6 to 13 Paul continues to show that prophecy is superior to tongue-speaking. Though Paul did have the gift of tongues (see v. 18), he indicates that it would not

gift of the Spirit whereby a person was enabled to transmit messages from God and, occasionally, to predict the future (e.g., Agabus; see Acts 11:27, 28; 21:10, 11). In other words, we may not identify this gift with what we might call today a gift for preaching or Bible teaching. There is, however, a parallel between the gift of prophecy and that of preaching or teaching: both types of gifts enable the possessor to enrich the congregation spiritually without the need for an interpreter. Since others are told to "judge" or "discern" what the prophets say (v. 29), we gather that the utterances of the prophets had to be in harmony with revealed truth. Further, Paul requires that the prophets acknowledge that the things Paul writes are the commandments of the Lord (v. 37). It therefore seems clear "that the prophets were not sources of new truth to the church, but expounders of truth otherwise revealed" (J. A. Motyer, "Prophecy, Prophets," in *The New Bible Dictionary*, p. 1045). We are therefore justified, I believe, in concluding that Paul would consider the gift of preaching or Bible teaching today a more useful gift than that of speaking in tongues.

[64] *Commentary on Corinthians*, trans. John Pringle (Grand Rapids: Eerdmans, 1948), I, 434 (on I Cor. 14:1).

be profitable for any church if he would come to it speaking with tongues (v. 6). He compares tongue-speaking to the playing of musical instruments in such a way that there is no distinction between the sounds (v. 7), or to the blowing of a bugle in such a way that no one knows to what the bugler is calling (v. 8). One who speaks only in tongues is wasting his breath; he is speaking into the air (v. 9). "Paul here uses a very sharp expression, so that the very last Christian in Corinth who is still overrating the gift may finally be shaken awake out of his error."[65] Another figure is added: tongue-speaking is as useless in the church as a conversation between two people, neither of whom understands a word of what the other is saying (vv. 10 and 11). The conclusion is obvious: Let the tongue-speaker pray that he may interpret, since without interpretation his gift is useless in the church (v. 13).

In the next section, verses 14-19, Paul is apparently combating the view of some of the Corinthians that worship while one's understanding is quiescent is to be preferred to worship that involves the full use of one's intellectual powers. There seem to have been those in Corinth who thought that one could somehow get closer to God and penetrate more deeply into the supernatural world by leaving his understanding in abeyance — which happened when one spoke in tongues — than by using his understanding. Paul indicates, however, that this is a serious error. If I pray in a tongue, he says, apparently still discussing what one might do in a public worship service, my spirit prays but my understanding is unfruitful (v. 14). This type of prayer, however, is not to be preferred to prayer which involves the understanding: "I will pray with

<hr>

65 E. Krajewski, *Geistesgaben*, pp. 45-46 [translation mine]. See his illuminating discussion of this entire section of the chapter, pp. 44-47.

the spirit, and I will pray with the understanding also"
(v. 15). I believe Paul here means to say: I will pray in
church with my understanding, in a language which every
worshiper can understand. When I do this, I will still be
praying with my spirit (the spirit which would be exclusive-
ly active if I prayed only in tongues), but I will be praying
with my understanding also.[66] This is far better, because
now the unlearned person who happens to be in church
can say Amen when I give thanks, since he knows what I
said in prayer. The whole matter is again summarized in
verse 17: by prayer in tongues others are not edified. Therefore it is not true that one worships best in church when
his understanding is held in abeyance.

We pause now for a moment at verse 18, often quoted
by Pentecostals as underscoring their high estimate of the
gift of tongues: "I thank my God, I speak with tongues
more than ye all." Why, so say our Pentecostal friends,
would Paul thank God for this gift if it had no value?
The gift had value — this I do not deny. But Paul's whole
point in this chapter is to show that the gift of tongues
has a very limited value. Some avid tongue-speaker in Corinth, however, might try to discredit what Paul was saying
about tongues by contending that Paul himself did not
possess this gift, and therefore could not be expected to
comment favorably about it. Paul meets this possible ob-
jection by reminding the Corinthians that he did indeed
possess the gift — that, in fact, he spoke with tongues more

---

[66] Another possible interpretation of these words is: I will keep on
praying in tongues in church services, but I will also pray in a known
language right after I have prayed in tongues, so that people will know
what I said when I prayed in tongues. I do not believe that this interpretation is the correct one, however, since Paul's main purpose
in this section of the chapter is to discourage praying in tongues at
church services. Further, note what he says in verse 19 about his re-
luctance to use tongue-speaking in a church service.

than they did. In view of this fact, his devaluation of tongues is all the more significant: "Yet in the church I had rather speak five words with my understanding, that by my voice I might teach others also, than ten thousand words in an unknown tongue" (v. 19). Again the thrust of the argument is: to speak in a language the people can understand is far better and far more edifying to the church than to speak in tongues. These words were said, the reader is reminded, not by one who had had no experience with tongues, but by one who spoke with tongues more than the Corinthians did! It is almost as if the most noted Pentecostal leader in the world would visit all the Pentecostal churches and say to them, "Brethren, you know that I speak with tongues more than all of you do. Yet I strongly advise you not to exercise this gift in the church service, but rather to speak in the language your people can understand, since this is far better for the church!"[67]

It would seem that Paul is suggesting that undue exaltation of the gift of tongues is an evidence of spiritual immaturity, since he opens the next section of the chapter (vv. 20-25) by saying, "Brethren, be not children in understanding." In the next four verses the familiar point is made again: prophecy is far superior to tongues.

[67] Brumback tries to tone down the devaluation of tongues here given by saying that what Paul meant to disparage was glossolalia without interpretation. When tongues are interpreted, however, so Brumback continues, they are equal to prophecy, in view of the teaching of I Cor. 14:5 (*op. cit.*, p. 161; see also p. 45). I would counter by observing that the entire section of I Corinthians under discussion is devoted to a demonstration of the superiority of prophecy over tongues — even over interpreted tongues (see the comparative listing of prophecy and interpretation of tongues in 12:10). Besides, it is precisely Paul, who speaks with tongues more than all the Corinthians, and who presumably could find people who could interpret for him, who says, "I had rather speak five words with my understanding (that is, not in a tongue, even though that tongue should be interpreted) . . . than ten thousand words in an unknown tongue."

From verse 21 we learn that strange tongues did not succeed in bringing the Israelites to repentance in Old Testament times. From verse 23 we learn that tongue-speaking in New Testament times, even when done by a whole church full of people, will only lead unbelievers to say, "These have lost their minds!" Verses 24 and 25 make the point that the exercise of the gift of prophecy is far more likely to lead an unbeliever to repent than the exercise of glossolalia.

Having set forth the comparative values of prophecy and glossolalia in verses 1-25, Paul now goes on to give some directions for public meetings (vv. 26-33). He recognizes that in the Corinthian Church various people have various spiritual gifts. We have in these verses an interesting picture of the nature of worship services in the early church. "When ye come together, every one of you [or each one, ASV] hath a psalm, hath a doctrine [or teaching, ASV], hath a tongue, hath a revelation, hath an interpretation" (v. 26). Apparently, therefore, various members of the church were ready to exercise their gifts in the service. Paul insists, however, that "all things be done unto edifying" (v. 26). The main purpose in the exercise of any spiritual gift may never be the enhancement of the prestige of the worshiper, or even his own edification, but must always be the edification of the church.

Of particular interest to us now is what Paul says here about the exercise of the gift of tongues. He does not rule tongue-speaking out altogether, but he permits it only under very definite restrictions. Not more than two or three people are to speak in tongues at any one meeting; these are not to speak at the same time but in turn ("by course" in the King James Version); and every utterance in tongues is to be followed by an interpretation (v. 27). If there is no interpreter present, no one is to speak with tongues in the service (v. 28). It will be noted that Paul definitely forbids certain types of tongue-speaking: tongue-speaking which is done from fleshly motives, which is done only to enhance one's own prestige, which is done so as to cause confusion in the service, and which is done without an interpretation. It will also be noted that Paul only permits such tongue-speaking as will edify the church.

Pentecostals rightly observe that restrictions are here also imposed on prophecy: prophets, too, are to speak by two or three (v. 29). Brumback argues on the basis of this restriction that Paul is therefore not really placing prophecy higher than interpreted tongues.[68] Though it is correct to say that similar limitations are here imposed on tongue-speakers and prophets, it remains true that the basic thrust of chapter 14 was to place a higher value on prophecy than on glossolalia. The fact that both tongue-speaking and prophecy are permitted in the church service, though under definite restrictions, by no means invalidates the main point of the entire chapter: the superiority of prophecy to tongues.

Paul summarizes in verse 39: "Wherefore, my brethren, desire earnestly to prophesy, and forbid not to speak with tongues" (ASV). Pentecostals are very fond of quoting the last clause as giving much support to their cause. We must, of course, grant them the point that Paul does not forbid tongue-speaking. What was implied in the previous argumentation, however, was that we cannot expect that everybody has received or shall receive this gift. And what has been the primary stress throughout the chapter, and is still implied in the words of verse 39, is that the gift of prophecy is to be more earnestly desired than the gift of tongues. For though the statement about tongue-speaking

68 *Op. cit.,* pp. 161, 169.

is negatively phrased ("forbid not"), Paul's positive injunction is "desire earnestly to prophesy."

The conclusion to be drawn from our examination of I Corinthians 12 to 14 is that Paul here definitely does not attach as high a value to the gift of tongues as do Pentecostals and Neo-Pentecostals today. It appears that when the Corinthians made a list of spiritual gifts, glossolalia was at the top, whereas in Paul's listings it is at the bottom. Paul rebukes the mentality which sees in the ability to speak with tongues the sign of an exceptionally significant spiritual achievement. Glossolalia is by no means the highest gift of the Spirit, so Paul teaches here, for, first, prophecy is a more valuable gift than tongues and, second, the cultivation of love is far more important than the exercise of either tongues or prophecy. Apart from love, in fact, all special gifts of the Spirit are useless (I Cor. 13:1-3).

As was previously observed, neither do these chapters give any support whatever to the doctrine that glossolalia is the indispensable evidence of one's having received the baptism with the Holy Spirit. If that doctrine were true, one would expect Paul somewhere to interrupt his discussion of spiritual gifts by saying something like this: "I know that the Spirit will not give you all the gift of tongues. But you realize, of course, that you must all speak with tongues at least once in your lives as evidence that you have received the baptism with the Holy Spirit. You might not keep on speaking with tongues after that, but you must all try to do this at least once. For you cannot have any assurance that you are really filled with the Spirit of God unless you have spoken with tongues." There is, however, nothing of this sort in Paul's writings, and there is nothing of this sort in these chapters. Surely, if Paul accepted the doctrine under discussion, he would have said something about it in these chapters, the only chapters in which he expounds the significance of tongue-speaking.

As a matter of fact, I Corinthians 12-14, when soberly considered, rather provides evidence that the above-mentioned doctrine is not true. For, whereas Pentecostals tell us that tongue-speaking is a sign that a believer has received his Spirit-baptism,[69] Paul specifically says in chapter 14:20 that tongues are a sign "not to them that believe, but to them that believe not." Further, the burden of the entire discussion of glossolalia in these chapters is that the surest proof of being filled with the Spirit is to abound in love toward one another. In fact, rather than to suggest that the ability to speak with tongues is a sign of mature, full-grown Christianity, Paul intimates quite the opposite thought. The Corinthian Church is the only New Testament church which we know to have contained many tongue-speakers; and yet it is precisely the Corinthians whom Paul addressed as "babes in Christ" and as being "yet carnal" (I Corinthians 3:1, 3). One would have a difficult time proving that those who spoke with tongues at Corinth were exceptions to whom these characterizations did not apply, since Paul implies in chapters 12-14 that the tongue-speakers were responsible for much of the confusion and lack of mutual edification that was present in this church.

As we have seen, Pentecostals build their case for Spirit-baptism evidenced by glossolalia on the accounts of tongue-speaking found in the book of Acts. They then turn to I Corinthians, not to find support for Spirit-baptism, but to find Scriptural validation for their exercise of the gift of tongues, carefully distinguishing between the gift of tongues and tongues as the initial sign of Spirit-baptism. Actually, however, should not the procedure have been reversed? If one wishes to know the doctrinal teaching

---

[69] "The initial physical sign," Art. 8 of the Assemblies of God *Fundamental Truths*.

of the New Testament, should one go first to a historical book like Acts? The epistles, in distinction from Acts, are primary sources of doctrinal instruction. The First Epistle to the Corinthians, as we saw, does not in any way confirm the teaching that every believer must undergo a Spirit-baptism subsequent to and distinct from regeneration, which baptism is to be evidenced by tongue-speaking. And I Corinthians is the only New Testament epistle which deals with the question of glossolalia! Should this not settle the matter? In the book of Acts Luke narrates the history of the early New Testament church. His primary purpose is not to teach doctrine but to recount history. Is it hermeneutically justifiable, then, to use the book of Acts as the primary source for a central doctrine of the church — particularly when, according to a prominent Pentecostal writer's own admission,[70] the doctrine alleged to be taught in the book of Acts is not supported by Paul's teaching in I Corinthians?

One more point needs to be taken up before we leave the Corinthians material. Do these chapters of I Corinthians justify the use of glossolalia for devotional purposes? This is often asserted by Pentecostals[71] and Neo-Pentecostals. The latter group, who do not encourage tongue-speaking in church services, lay most of their stress on the value of glossolalia for private devotions and for small group meetings.

By way of reply, it must first be admitted that Paul does not forbid glossolalia. Yet he recommends prophecy above tongues because prophecy is of greater benefit to the congregation, and because the law of love would sug-

---

[70] Brumback, *op. cit.*, p. 266: "In I Corinthians 12 to 14 there is not the slightest hint that the gift of tongues is associated, in any direct sense, with the filling with the Holy Spirit. . . ."

[71] E.g., in Brumback, *op. cit.*, pp. 291-98; Riggs, *op. cit.*, p. 165; and Williams, *op. cit.*, III, 49.

gest that we should be more eager to engage in what benefits the congregation than in what is of benefit only to ourselves. One who would be more concerned to cultivate a gift by which he himself would be edified than one by which the congregation might be edified would be guilty of a kind of spiritual self-centeredness.

It must further be observed that Paul nowhere actually tells his readers that they must all seek the gift of tongues. Pentecostals often point to I Corinthians 14:5a as teaching this: "I would that ye all spake with tongues." But this first clause should not be torn out of its context. When read together with the rest of the verse, these words convey a quite different impression: "I would that ye all spake with tongues, but rather that ye prophesied: for greater is he that prophesieth than he that speaketh with tongues. . . ." And in verse 39, where he summarizes his entire discussion, Paul, while not forbidding tongues, positively enjoins prophecy: "Wherefore, my brethren, desire earnestly to prophesy, and forbid not to speak with tongues" (ASV).

Brumback quotes with approval I Corinthians 14:4, "He that speaketh in an unknown tongue edifieth himself," as justifying glossolalia for personal edification.[72] Yet the total thrust of verses 4-5, which should be read together, is to make tongue-speaking less desirable than prophesying: "He that speaketh in an unknown tongue edifieth himself; but he that prophesieth edifieth the church. I would that ye all spake with tongues, but rather that ye prophesied. . . ." According to this passage edifying oneself is far inferior to edifying the church; hence one should rather seek the higher gift.

Pentecostals often quote I Corinthians 14:14 and 15

[72] *Op. cit.,* pp. 168, 298.

as justifying the use of glossolalia for devotional purposes.[73] As we saw, however, Paul is here probably discussing the use of tongues in a public worship service rather than the devotional use of tongues. Further, the more likely interpretation of verse 15 is not that Paul favors praying in tongues in a church service, but rather that he favors praying in a known language, so that both his spirit and his understanding may be active.

Pentecostals contend, as we have seen, that one who speaks in tongues does not understand what he is saying. On the basis of the general teaching of Scripture on prayer, one may well ask whether we have any assurance that devotional prayer in tongues is superior to devotional prayer in one's own language. What is the value of praying in tongues for private devotions if one does not know what he is praying for? As a matter of fact, if one does not know what he is saying at the time, how can he be certain that he is praying at all? The Bible teaches us to pray for such things as food (Matt. 6:11), forgiveness of sins (Matt. 6:12), wisdom (Jas. 1:5), strength (Eph. 3:16), and so on. But how can one specifically ask for these things in prayer if he does not know what he is saying when he prays? When Christ taught His disciples how to pray, he did not teach them to pray in an unknown tongue, but rather gave them a model prayer in the language which they understood (Matt. 6:9-13, Luke 11:2-4). What ground do we have for concluding that a prayer which we do not ourselves understand could be superior to the prayer our Lord taught us?

We conclude that, though Paul in these chapters from I Corinthians does assign some value to glossolalia, this value is quite carefully circumscribed. One certainly does

---

[73] Brumback, *op. cit.*, pp. 291-92; Frodsham, *op. cit.* (1946 ed.), p. 269.

not get the impression from these chapters that tongue-speaking is the *sine qua non* of mature Christianity — the gift which is indispensable for vibrant personal devotions, warm and fervent intercession, or full-orbed victorious Christian living. The predominant impression one receives from a careful study of these chapters is rather that if one is seeking the very best gifts, he will probably not seek glossolalia.

4

A Theological Evaluation of Tongue-Speaking

W E HAVE NOW LOOKED AT CERTAIN SPECIFIC BIBLE passages on which Pentecostals base their contention that every believer ought to seek the baptism with the Holy Spirit which is initially evidenced by speaking with tongues, and have found that the Biblical evidence to which they appeal does not support their teaching. Let us now go on to look at glossolalia in the light of the teachings of the entire Bible, and in the light of the theological heritage of historic Christianity. In other words, as we have made a Biblical evaluation of glossolalia, let us now evaluate the tongue-speaking movement from a theological point of view. I should like to make this analysis by means of a series of statements which embody theological judgments.

1. *It cannot be proved with finality that the miraculous gifts of the Spirit, which include tongue-speaking, are still in the church today.*

When one examines the list of spiritual gifts found in I Corinthians 12:8-10 and 28, it becomes quite clear that some of these gifts were miraculous in nature. Certainly "the gifts of healing" (*charismata iamatōn,* v. 9) and "the working of miracles" or "workings of miracles" (*energēmata dunameōn,* v. 10) fall into this category, and probably a number of the others. Many writers, in fact (like John Owen and Charles Hodge), affirm that the entire list of spiritual gifts found in I Corinthians 12:8-10 consists of supernatural or miraculous gifts. A distinction commonly made within the category of spiritual gifts is that of ordinary and extraordinary gifts of the Spirit. When we look at the list of gifts given in Romans 12:6-8, for example, we get the impression that Paul was there enumerating the ordinary gifts of the Spirit, gifts which did not necessarily involve a supernatural or miraculous element: prophecy, ministry, teaching, exhorting, giving, ruling, showing mercy.[1] It is also significant that in another listing of the offices given by Christ to His church, the one found in Ephesians 4:11, there is no mention of healings, miracles, tongues, or interpretations of tongues.

It is admitted by both Pentecostals and non-Pentecostals that the gift of tongues (as well as the companion gift of interpretation) was a supernatural or extraordinary gift. And this, of course, immediately raises the question: Did these extraordinary gifts of the Spirit remain in the church after the apostolic period? John Owen, whose "Discourse of Spiritual Gifts" in his monumental work on the Holy Spirit is the most thorough treatment of the subject I could find, expresses the opinion of most conservative Protestant theologians when he says:

---

[1] If *prophecy* be here understood as a miraculous gift which involved the ability to receive direct revelations from God, it would be an exception to the statement made above. It is possible, however, that the word *prophecy* as here used means simply the gift of preaching the word, since the other gifts mentioned in the immediate context are not of the supernatural or miraculous type.

> Nor have we any undoubted testimony that any of those
> gifts which were truly *miraculous,* and every way above the
> faculties of men, were communicated unto any after the
> expiration of the generation of them who conversed
> with Christ in the flesh, or those who received the Holy
> Ghost by their ministry.[2]

He asserts on a later page that these miraculous gifts
were necessary in order to gain a hearing for the gospel
when it was first proclaimed, since only by such demon-
strations of miraculous power could the prejudices of
men be overcome.[3]

Benjamin B. Warfield's position on these miraculous
gifts of the Spirit, or charismata, as they are often called,
may also be noted. He maintains that these special gifts
of the Spirit, including tongue-speaking, were given to
authenticate the apostles as messengers from God.[4] Not
only did the apostles possess these gifts, they also were able
to bestow them on others. There is no record, Warfield
continues, of the bestowing of these gifts on someone by
the laying on of the hands of any one other than an apostle.[5]
Hence Warfield concludes that these gifts passed out of
the church after the apostles died:

> They [these miraculous gifts] were part of the credentials
> of the Apostles as the authoritative agents of God in
> founding the church. Their function thus confined them
> to distinctively the Apostolic Church, and they necessarily
> passed away with it.[6]

[2] *On the Holy Spirit* (Philadelphia: Protestant Episcopal Book
Society, 1862) , Part II, pp. 474-75.

[3] *Ibid.,* pp. 478-86.

[4] *Miracles Yesterday and Today,* p. 21.

[5] *Ibid.,* p. 22. The case of the Samaritans is particularly cited by
way of confirmation, since in Samaria the special gifts of the Spirit
were not bestowed until after the apostles had come down from
Jerusalem (p. 23) .

[6] *Ibid.,* p. 6.

How, now, do our Pentecostal friends answer these objections to the continuance of tongues? Earlier we noted their appeal to Mark 16:17-18 and I Corinthians 12:28 as teaching that the gift of tongues was intended to remain in the church, and we have seen that these passages do not compel us to accept that conclusion. Brumback further states that we have no "definite declaration by the Lord of His intention to cause tongues and other powers to cease shortly after the establishing of the Church."[7] This is true enough. But is this compelling proof? In the Sermon on the Mount Jesus gave instructions about the proper way of offering gifts at the altar — an obvious reference to Jewish modes of worship. Nowhere do we read specifically that He abolished the Jewish altar and its sacrifices — yet we are certain that this mode of worship is no longer required today. In I Corinthians 12:28, furthermore, where the gift of tongues is mentioned, Paul asserts that God has set apostles in the church. Yet our Pentecostal friends agree that this passage does not compel us to affirm that there must be men in the church today who hold the office of apostle. How, then, can they be certain that when Paul speaks here of "divers kinds of tongues" we may be sure that there are still people in the church today who possess this special endowment of the Spirit?

There are, I believe, some weighty considerations for holding that special gifts of the Spirit, like tongue-speaking, are no longer operative in the church today. Let us look at some of these considerations:[8]

---

[7] *What Meaneth This?*, p. 61.

[8] Incidentally, I do not believe that one can justifiably appeal in this connection to I Cor. 13:8, "whether there be tongues, they shall cease." For the same verse tells us that prophecies and knowledge shall also cease, and the succeeding context makes it quite clear that the contrast here is not between the apostolic age and the succeeding

(a) Certain Scripture passages specifically associate the miraculous gifts of the Spirit with the work of the apostles. The first of these to which we turn our attention is Acts 14:3, "Long time therefore abode they speaking boldly in the Lord, which gave testimony unto the word of his grace, and granted signs and wonders to be done by their hands." These words describe the activities of Paul and Barnabas in Iconium during Paul's first missionary journey. Note that these signs and wonders were granted by God to these apostles[9] in order to confirm the gospel message they were bringing. The American Standard Version is here a little more precise than the King James: "speaking boldly in the Lord, who bare witness unto the word of his grace, granting signs and wonders to be done by their hands." In the Greek the dative participle *didonti* (giving) follows the dative participle *marturounti* (witnessing) by way of explication. The meaning of the sentence is, in other words, that God bore witness to (or gave testimony to) the word of His grace by granting signs and wonders to be done by their hands. The wonders the apostles did constituted a testimony from God that they were truly God's messengers.

As we have seen, the church at Corinth was richly endowed with the special gifts of the Spirit. It is highly significant to note that in Paul's second letter to the Corinthians, probably written soon after the first, he wrote, "Truly the signs of an apostle were wrought among you in all patience, in signs, and wonders, and mighty deeds" (II Cor. 12:12). In the context Paul is vindicating his apostleship. To prove that he was indeed an apostle,

---

era, but rather between the period before the Second Coming of Christ and the period after the Second Coming "when that which is perfect is come" (v. 10).

9 Barnabas is also called an apostle in verse 14.

Paul here reminds his readers of the signs, wonders, and mighty deeds which were done through him, calling these manifestations of the power of the Spirit "signs of an apostle." Does not this passage strongly suggest that the special gifts of the Spirit were not intended to continue in the church, but were signs authenticating the apostles, as Warfield contends?

We find another reference to the authenticating significance of the special charismata in Romans 15:15-19:

> But I write the more boldly unto you in some measure, as putting you again in remembrance, because of the grace that was given me of God, that I should be a minister of Christ Jesus unto the Gentiles, ministering the gospel of God, that the offering up of the Gentiles might be made acceptable, being sanctified by the Holy Spirit. I have therefore my glorying in Christ Jesus in things pertaining to God. For I will not dare to speak of any things save those which Christ wrought through me, for the obedience of the Gentiles, by word and deed, in the power of signs and wonders, in the power of the Holy Spirit; so that from Jerusalem, and round about even unto Illyricum, I have fully preached the gospel of Christ (ASV).

Paul here reminds the brethren at Rome that it was through the grace of God that he was made a minister of Christ to the Gentiles, and that therefore he glories in Christ Jesus rather than in himself. He goes on to remind his readers of the things which Christ wrought through him for the obedience of the Gentiles "by word and deed, in the power of signs and wonders, in the power of the Holy Spirit." It is clear that the signs and wonders Paul was permitted to perform were means whereby Christ enabled him to bring the Gentiles to obedience, and were thus inseparably connected with his ministry as the apostle to the Gentiles.

Very clear light is shed on the question of the purpose of the special gifts of the Spirit by Hebrews 2:3 and 4:

> How shall we escape, if we neglect so great salvation; which at the first began to be spoken by the Lord, and was confirmed unto us by them that heard him;
>
> God also bearing them witness, both with signs and wonders, and with divers miracles, and gifts of the Holy Ghost, according to his own will?

According to this passage the word of salvation was first spoken by the Lord Jesus Christ Himself. It was then confirmed to both the writer and the readers of this epistle by those who heard the Lord. "Them that heard him" could designate either the apostles or a wider circle than the apostles; the reference to signs and wonders in the next verse, however, makes it rather likely that the apostles are here meant. The tense of the participle in verse 4, which is rendered "bearing witness," is present, indicating that the witness about to be described was a continuing one. How, now, did God bear witness with the apostles to the authenticity of the gospel message? By "signs and wonders, and with divers miracles, and gifts of the Holy Ghost" (v. 4). The last word, translated *gifts,* literally means *distributions (merismois)*; it clearly refers to the various gifts of the Holy Spirit such as are described in I Corinthians 12, and undoubtedly includes glossolalia. The function, then, of all these special gifts or charismata of the Spirit is here described as one of confirmation: God continually bore witness with the apostles through these gifts, and thereby confirmed the message of salvation to the second-generation readers of the Epistle to the Hebrews.

From the passages just discussed we learn that the purpose and function of the special miraculous gifts of the Spirit was to authenticate the apostles as true messengers from God, and thus to confirm the gospel of salvation. This being the case, we can understand why these miraculous signs should be so much in evidence in apostolic times. But, this being the case, we can also understand why these miraculous signs should disappear when the apostles passed from the scene. If the miraculous signs were intended to authenticate the apostles, they would not longer be needed after the apostles had done their work.

Our Pentecostal friends, however, like to say: These special miraculous gifts of the Spirit are still needed today for the purpose of evangelism.

> . . . The Church, in its scrutiny of early church methods of evangelization, has overlooked a most vital part, viz., divine confirmation of the message with miraculous signs. The failure of the Church since apostolic days to seek and receive such confirmation is a major factor in her slowness in carrying out the Great Commission.[10]

It is argued here that if a church is able to manifest miraculous phenomena like glossolalia it will attract much more attention and be much more blessed in its evangelistic and missionary program than when these phenomena are missing. The answer to this claim, however, is precisely this: the church today no longer needs this kind of confirmation of the message. In the days of the apostles it was necessary for the message to be confirmed by miraculous signs. But today we have the complete Bible, including the entire New Testament. To contend that the church still needs miraculous signs to confirm the gospel message is, it seems to me, to overlook the finality of Scripture. The words of Abraham to the rich man in the parable may be recalled here: "If they [the rich man's brothers] hear not Moses and the prophets, neither will they be persuaded, though one rose from the dead" (Luke 16:31).

(b) The way Paul treats glossolalia in I Corinthians 12 to 14 suggests that this gift is no longer urgently needed in the church. Paul, as we have seen, definitely plays down tongue-speaking in these chapters. The main

---

[10] Brumback, *op. cit.*, p. 323.

burden of his discussion is that the gift of prophecy is to be sought far more earnestly than the gift of tongues. He makes it abundantly clear that in church services prophecy is to be preferred to tongue-speaking. Though he permits a restricted use of glossolalia in the service, even such tongue-speaking as he allows must be interpreted. A person studying this letter carefully would soon gather from Paul's remarks that the congregation would be edified most if whatever message was to be given to it would be given through prophecy rather than through tongues, and that it would therefore be far better if the procedure of speaking in a tongue and then having that tongue interpreted were simply eliminated.

As far as witnessing to people outside the church is concerned, Paul does say that tongues are a sign, not to them that believe but to them that believe not. So glossolalia does have some value in attesting the genuineness of the gospel message to unbelievers. Yet even for the purpose of witnessing to unbelievers, Paul goes on to say in these chapters, prophecy is superior to tongue-speaking. For it is far more likely that an unbeliever will be brought to the faith by means of prophecy than by means of tongues (chap. 14:24, 25).

I am not contending that God could not have continued the gift of glossolalia in the church, if He had been pleased to do so. I am only saying that the very limited value which Paul ascribes to this gift in I Corinthians 12 to 14 suggests that there would seem to be little point in having this gift continued.

(c) The fact that there is no reference to glossolalia in any New Testament epistle other than I Corinthians also strongly suggests that this gift was not intended to remain in the church. If God had intended to keep glossolalia in the church, particularly if this gift was to remain a rich channel of blessing for the church, one would expect that there would be some reference to it in other New Testament epistles besides I Corinthians. But we find no such reference. Though in I Corinthians Paul does discuss glossolalia, as we saw, he never once refers to it again in any other letter of his. From the book of Acts we learn that all the apostles spoke with tongues on the Day of Pentecost. Yet we find no reference whatever to glossolalia in the epistles written by James, Peter, John, Jude, and the author of Hebrews. Though there are many references in these letters to the work of the Spirit, the witness of the Spirit, and the fruit of the Spirit, there is no reference to speaking with tongues.

It is, further, highly significant that the ability to speak with tongues is never mentioned among the qualifications for elders or bishops and deacons in I Timothy 3:1-13 and Titus 1:5-9. Surely if the gift of tongues were to remain in the church, one would have expected to find it a required qualification for office-bearers! The fact that the pastoral epistles just mentioned were written considerably later than I Corinthians suggests that already by this time glossolalia may have been disappearing from the church.

(d) The almost total absence of glossolalia in the history of the church from A.D. 100 to 1900 is hardly compatible with the claim that God intended the gift of tongues to remain in the church. We have seen above that there are very few reports of tongue-speaking in the history of the church during those years. Some of the reports we have are of questionable authenticity; others concern groups which were definitely heretical, like the Montanists. Even if all the reports of glossolalia during these years were true, the groups which practiced tongue-speaking would still be few and far between. It simply cannot be denied that, speaking by and large, tongue-speaking was virtually unknown in the major bodies of Christendom until about 1900.

I realize that the argument from history is not absolutely compelling. It is, of course, conceivable that God, for reasons best known to Himself, decided to deprive His church of glossolalia for eighteen centuries and then, at the beginning of the twentieth century, once again to restore this gift to the church. But when it is contended, as is done by Pentecostals, that a church which does not manifest glossolalia is missing one of the richest avenues of blessing God has provided for His people,[11] we are indeed mystified by this long gap in the history of tongue-speaking. If tongue-speaking is as great a blessing to the church as our Pentecostal brothers claim it is, why was it virtually absent from the church between A.D. 100 and 1900? Did God deliberately impoverish His people?

The above considerations strongly suggest that miraculous gifts of the Spirit such as glossolalia are no longer present in the church today. Can our Pentecostal friends prove with finality, both from the Scriptures and from the history of the church, that these miraculous gifts are still with us?

2. *The distinctive doctrine of Pentecostal churches which is basic to their teachings on glossolalia, namely, that every believer must seek a postconversion Spirit-baptism, has no basis in Scripture.*

We have already seen that the passages in the book of Acts to which Pentecostals commonly appeal do not support this doctrine. Does this doctrine obtain any support from other Scriptural passages? On the contrary, the teaching that a regenerated person must still undergo a

11 Brumback, *op. cit.,* pp. 291, 324-32.

baptism of the Spirit whereby he then receives the fulness of the Spirit is based on a misunderstanding of the work of the Spirit. When the Spirit regenerates us, He enters into our lives, not just as a power but as a Person. Paul expresses this thought very clearly in Romans 8:9, "Ye [regenerate people, believers] are not in the flesh, but in the Spirit, if so be that the Spirit of God dwell in you." Paul adds in the next sentence, "Now if any man have not the Spirit of Christ, he is none of his." If one belongs to Christ, in other words, he has the Spirit of Christ, and if he has the Spirit of Christ, that Spirit is dwelling in him. What more, now, can the Spirit do but to dwell in him? Why should it be necessary for the Spirit to be bestowed upon such a person in a "second blessing" or "second work of grace" or "Spirit-baptism," when the Spirit is already *dwelling* within him? To the same effect is I Corinthians 3:16, "Know ye not that ye are the temple of God, and that the Spirit of God dwelleth in you?"

Nowhere in the New Testament, in fact, do we find believers asking for such a baptism with or in the Holy Spirit, and nowhere do we find the apostles instructing believers to seek such a baptism. Rather, we find Paul saying to the Galatians, "If we live in the Spirit, let us also walk in the Spirit" (Gal. 5:25). The implication is clear: if we have been born again, we have the Spirit, since only the Spirit can regenerate us. If this be so, Paul urges, then in or by that same Spirit in whom we live let us also walk. Paul does not say: wait for a baptism with the Spirit so that you will be able to walk in Him. He says: Walk more fully in or by that Spirit whom you have, who has already given you a new heart, in whom you already live.

It is, of course, true that we need to strive constantly for a greater infilling with or surrender to the Spirit. But this does not mean that after we have been regenerated we must now wait for the Spirit to make the next move. Rather, if I may be permitted to put it that way, the next move is up to us: we must yield ourselves more fully to that Spirit who already dwells within.[12] This, as we have seen, is the thrust of Ephesians 5:18, "And be not drunk with wine, wherein is excess; but be filled with the Spirit." The present tense of the imperative, *plērousthe,* means: be continually filled, keep on being filled. The passage points to a lifelong striving, not just to a momentary experience. Neither is Paul implying that the readers of the Epistle to the Ephesians do not yet have the Spirit, for in 1:13 he had written, "in whom [Christ], having also believed, ye were sealed with the Holy Spirit of promise" (ASV).

We must reluctantly conclude, therefore, that the theology of Pentecostalism is in this respect based more upon experience than upon Scripture. As Russell T. Hitt, editor of *Eternity* magazine, puts it,

> We must judge all teaching by the Word of God. Many who have had a recent Pentecostal experience have trouble giving a proper scriptural explanation for what has happened. Instead they testify to an experience, and build up a strange framework of doctrine from the book of Acts for the questionable doctrine of "the baptism in the Spirit."[13]

But we may not base doctrine primarily upon experience. I have heard Mormons say that they were convinced that Joseph Smith was a true prophet of God because they had had a wonderful spiritual experience in the Mormon religion. If experience is basic to doctrine, how could

---

[12] I am not here suggesting that we can yield ourselves more fully to the Holy Spirit in our own strength. We can only do this in God's strength (John 15:5, Phil. 4:13). But my point is: we do not need to wait for some specific additional Spirit-baptism experience before we can surrender ourselves fully to the Spirit.

[13] "The New Pentecostalism," *Eternity,* July, 1963, reprint, p. 7.

we ever prove the Mormons wrong — or, for that matter, Buddhists, Hindus, or Moslems?

3. *The theology of Pentecostalism erroneously teaches that a spiritual blessing must be attested to by a physical phenomenon.*

Speaking with tongues, it is said, is the initial physical sign of having been baptized in the Holy Spirit. But how can a physical sign be proof of a spiritual state? Pentecostals point to the four instances in the book of Acts where tongue-speaking proved that the Spirit had been received in His fullness (though in the case of the Samaritans tongues are not actually mentioned), but these instances were associated either with Pentecost or with an extension of Pentecost, as we have seen; and, further, there are a great many instances in the book of Acts where no mention is made of tongues, even in cases where we are told that people were filled with the Holy Spirit. Even Pentecostals admit, moreover, that the tongue-speaking which occurred in Corinth had nothing directly to do with being filled with the Spirit![14] How, then, can our Pentecostal friends affirm with such certainty that tongue-speaking today is the indispensable evidence of Spirit-baptism?

Does not the Bible itself indicate that the proof of being filled with the Spirit is not physical but spiritual? What does Paul say about this matter in Galatians 5:22-23? "But the fruit of the Spirit is love, joy, peace, longsuffering, gentleness, goodness, faith [faithfulness, ASV], meekness, temperance." One of the great dangers of Pentecostalism and Neo-Pentecostalism, it seems to me, is that people may become more concerned about the gifts of the Spirit than about the fruit of the Spirit. On the negative side, our Lord Himself said that even prophesying or

[14] Brumback, *op. cit.*, p. 266.

miracle-working do not in themselves prove that a person is truly filled with the Spirit:

> Many will say to me in that day, Lord, Lord, have we not prophesied in thy name? and in thy name have cast out devils? and in thy name done many wonderful works?
>
> And then will I profess unto them, I never knew you: depart from me, ye that work iniquity (Mt. 7:22-23).

Though Augustine wrote the following words more than 1500 years ago, they are as appropriate now as they must have been then:

> In the earliest times, "the Holy Ghost fell upon them that believed: and they spake with tongues," which they had not learned, "as the Spirit gave them utterance." These were signs adapted to the time. . . . If then the witness of the presence of the Holy Ghost be not now given through these miracles, by what is it given, by what does one get to know that he has received the Holy Ghost? Let him question his own heart. If he love his brother, the Spirit of God dwelleth in him.[15]

4. *Implicit in Pentecostalism is a kind of subordination of Christ to the Holy Spirit which is not in harmony with Scripture.*

We have noted earlier that Ralph M. Riggs describes the baptism of the Holy Spirit in terms which imply a kind of subordinationism:

> This experience [of Spirit-baptism] is as distinct from conversion as the Holy Spirit is distinct from Christ. His [the Spirit's] coming to the believer at the Baptism is the coming of the Third Person of the Trinity, in addition to the coming of Christ, which takes place at conversion.[16]

---

15 *Homilies on the First Epistle of John,* VI, 10; in *Nicene and Post-Nicene Fathers,* First Series, Vol. XII.

16 *The Spirit Himself,* pp. 79-80.

What is Riggs here saying? That conversion means *merely* the coming of Christ, but that Spirit-baptism means the coming of the Holy Spirit. Since one has not reached the highest rung on the spiritual ladder until he has received the Spirit-baptism, it is evident that merely to receive Christ is to remain on a low spiritual level.

At another place this same writer, after explaining that the Holy Spirit is the Personal Leader of the church, asks:

> How can we live and function effectively without our God-appointed Head and Leader? How disrupting and defeating to the plan and purpose of God if we do not co-operate at the outset of our Christian experience by receiving the fullness of the Holy Spirit Baptism![17]

The implication is clear: if one has not received the Spirit-baptism, one is living without his God-appointed Leader. He may have received Christ at the time of conversion, but he is still leaderless! To have merely Christ in his heart is to have an inferior, second-rate kind of Christianity!

How utterly at variance this is with the Bible! Christ teaches otherwise: "He [the Spirit] shall glorify me: for he shall receive of mine, and shall shew it unto you" (John 16:14). To exalt the work of the Spirit is praiseworthy, but to exalt the Spirit above Christ is an error comparable to the subordination of Christ to the Father of which the ancient Arians were guilty!

Kurt Hutten's comment is to the point:

> Pentecostal theology has absolutized the doctrine of the Holy Spirit. . . . By so doing it has denied the testimony of Scripture. For, according to Scripture, the crucified and risen one is and remains the midpoint that dominates and penetrates all else. And according to Scripture Christ and the Holy Spirit may not be torn apart; the work of the one may not be distinguished from that of the other in

[17] *Ibid.,* pp. 81-82.

quality or rank. There is no working of the Holy Spirit beyond the cross; there is only a working of the Spirit under the cross.[18]

5. *The theology of Pentecostalism tends to create two levels of Christians: those who have received the Spirit-baptism and those who have not.*

Pentecostals make it quite clear that people who have not received the baptism with the Holy Spirit have not attained the level of full-orbed Christian living. Pentecostal writers make a clear distinction between Spirit-baptism and conversion,[19] and between Spirit-baptism and sanctification.[20] Only Spirit-baptized persons are said to have been sealed with the Spirit,[21] and to have the earnest of the Spirit.[22] The baptism with the Holy Spirit is described as the coming of power from on high — a power that is called the *sine qua non* of Christian service.[23] This would imply that persons who have not received Spirit-baptism — the great majority of those who call themselves Christians — do not have adequate power for Christian service! Spirit-baptism is described by a Pentecostal writer as the coming of divine equipment for the battle against the devil;[24] the implication of this would seem to be that the vast army of ordinary, non-Pentecostal Christians are rushing into battle as unprepared, unarmed troops!

A little reflection will reveal how devastating this view of a two-level Christianity can be to the unity of the church. I am not charging Pentecostals with saying that a person cannot be saved without Spirit-baptism, but I am

---

18 *Seher, Gruebler, Enthusiasten,* 6th ed., p. 520 [translation mine].
19 Riggs, *op. cit.,* pp. 79-80.
20 P. C. Nelson, *Bible Doctrines,* p. 94.
21 Riggs, *op. cit.,* p. 73.
22 *Ibid.,* pp. 74-75.
23 *Ibid.,* p. 80.
24 *Ibid.,* p. 82.

observing that their theology leaves us with a great multitude of ordinary, garden-variety Christians, and a small group of elite Christians. How utterly untrue to Scripture! Paul says, in Galatians 3:28, "There can be neither Jew nor Greek, there can be neither bond nor free, there can be no male and female; for ye all are one man in Christ Jesus" (ASV). Pentecostals, however, ought to interrupt Paul at this juncture: "But, Paul, haven't you forgotten the distinction between believers who are Spirit-baptized and those who are not?" To suggest, further, that only Spirit-baptized people are sealed with the Spirit, have the earnest of the Spirit, and have been equipped with power from on high is to say that there are a number of New Testament passages that really have no message for the vast majority of believers since Apostolic days!

6. *The theology of Pentecostalism implies that the church has been without a leader, without adequate power, without full light, and without a full-orbed Christian experience from the end of the first century to the beginning of the twentieth.*

H. J. Stolee, in his *Speaking in Tongues,* originally published in 1936 and recently reprinted, says,

> It has always been a trait in fanatical movements to ignore and even deny the continuity of Christianity. The development of centuries is regarded virtually as a total failure.[25]

Sad to say, this tendency is also in evidence in Pentecostalism. Earlier we noted that, according to Pentecostal writers, the reason why glossolalia largely disappeared from the church during the centuries between A.D. 100 and 1900 was lack of faith on the part of God's people. Let us

[25] P. 97 (1963 ed.).

look into this matter a bit more closely. Carl Brumback argues that, though God could have held men responsible for the truth about Spirit-baptism during the entire era of church history since the Apostolic age, He did not apply His standards strictly during this entire period since His people, through their sin and failure, had rendered themselves incapable of conformity to those standards.[26] Many New Testament truths were plunged into almost total eclipse during the Middle Ages.[27] These truths were partly restored by the Reformation, but the Reformation did not go far enough. Certain portions of the truth were hidden from the Reformers, awaiting another hour for their full revelation.[28] Among the great truths which were not fully revealed to the Reformers was the doctrine of the baptism with the Holy Spirit.[29] At the dawn of the twentieth century the Lord saw fit to restore this truth to the church.[30] Before the twentieth century the experience of the post-Apostolic saints was not up to the Scriptural standard, because it was "not a full baptism with the Holy Ghost, not of a miraculous character, and not accompanied by tongues."[31]

What this amounts to saying is that during 1800 years of church history the entire church (with a few minor exceptions) failed to enjoy the fullness of Christian experience which God had intended His children to have! This means that giants like Calvin and Luther apparently did not have as much faith as Pentecostals do today. This means that, as we have seen, the church during all these years was really without a leader, without full power for

26 Brumback, *op. cit.*, pp. 276-77.
27 *Ibid.*, p. 277.
28 *Ibid.*, pp. 277-78.
29 *Ibid.*, p. 278.
30 *Ibid.*, p. 279.
31 *Ibid.*, p. 281.

service, and without the full light of God's truth. Not only so, but the greater part of the church today is similarly hampered, since it does not yet accept this latest truth God has revealed. The inescapable conclusion seems to be that Pentecostals alone are in full possession of God's truth; the rest of us will remain in partial darkness until we are ready to accept their teachings!

Does not this claim, however, deny the continued guidance of the Holy Spirit through eighteen centuries of church history? Does not this claim seriously jeopardize the truth of the universality of the church of Jesus Christ? Would not this claim seem to imply that only Pentecostals are God's true, Spirit-filled people? It is one thing to admit that all believers fall short of doing God's will and of fully understanding His revelation, but it is quite a different thing to claim that one's own group alone has the truth on this matter, while all other Christians are in error.

One might still ask whether the observations made in this chapter apply to Neo-Pentecostals as well as to Pentecostals. We do not, of course, have any systematic doctrinal books by Neo-Pentecostals which set forth what they all hold in common. Undoubtedly there is variation of opinion among Neo-Pentecostals, as there is among Pentecostals.

It is very well possible that many Neo-Pentecostals would not share the common Pentecostal position that glossolalia is *the* indispensable evidence that one has received Spirit-baptism. If so, some of the considerations advanced above would not apply to them. Yet, as has been shown, even the position that tongue-speaking is *an* evidence that one has been filled with the Holy Spirit is open to serious question.

It must be remembered, however, that Neo-Pentecostalism arose out of Pentecostalism; it would therefore be expected that on questions involving the significance and meaning of tongue-speaking, Neo-Pentecostals would have much in common with Pentecostals. We have noted, further, that a number of leading Neo-Pentecostals do take the common Pentecostal position on tongues. We have even seen that an official statement by the Board of Directors of the Blessed Trinity Society affirms that the baptism with the Holy Spirit is confirmed by tongue-speaking.[32] It would seem likely, therefore, that most Neo-Pentecostals, insofar as they have thought about the question, take the same position on the significance of glossolalia that Pentecostals do. To the extent that this is the case, the comments made in this chapter would apply to Neo-Pentecostals as well as to Pentecostals.

[32] See above, Chapter 2.

5

What We Can Learn from the Tongue-Speaking Movement

JUDGING FROM WHAT WE HAVE LEARNED ABOUT PENTE-costal doctrines so far, it would appear that our response both to Pentecostalism and Neo-Pentecostalism must be largely negative. Yet, as has been intimated before, there are many things which we can learn from this movement. In this final chapter, therefore, I propose to assess the positive aspects of both Pentecostalism and Neo-Pentecostalism, to see what challenge the tongue-speaking movement holds for the church today.

One of the most striking — and, for non-Pentecostals, most puzzling — aspects of the tongues movement is the fact that many people who have begun to speak with tongues report that this experience has been to them a source of great spiritual blessing. Carl Brumback, for instance, speaking for Pentecostals, states that there are few spiritual exercises more edifying to the individual believer than the gift of tongues when used in personal devotions.[1] Article 7 of the Assemblies of God *Statement*

1 *What Meaneth This?*, p. 291.

of Fundamental Truths asserts that the baptism in the Holy Spirit of which glossolalia is the initial evidence is followed by a deepened reverence for God, an intensified consecration to God and dedication to His work, and a more active love for Christ, for His Word, and for the lost. Morton Kelsey reports that all seven of the persons whose tongue-speaking experiences he describes in his book stated that this experience was one of the most valuable they had ever had.[2] Frequently it is said that the experiences culminating in glossolalia have transformed people's lives.[3] Periodicals like *Trinity* and *Voice* are filled with the personal testimonies of individuals who report that they have received a new lease on spiritual life through speaking in tongues.

What shall we say about all this? How are we to account for the present-day outburst of tongues? How are we to explain the spiritual invigoration glossolalia seems to have brought into the lives of so many people?

V. Raymond Edman, until recently president of Wheaton College, summed matters up pretty well when he said that there are really only three possibilities: Either glossolalia today is of the devil, or it is a genuine gift of the Spirit, or it is a phenomenon which, without being either primarily inspired by the devil or by the Spirit, has been psychologically induced.[4]

Is it possible that the tongue-speaking we are witnessing today has been demonically instigated? We certainly cannot rule out this possibility altogether. Satan, as Luther used to say, is the "ape of God," who often tries to imitate genuine works of the Spirit. We know from II Corinthians

2 *Tongue Speaking*, p. 4.

3 *Ibid.*, p. 2; Frank Farrell, "Outburst of Tongues," *Christianity Today*, VII, No. 24 (Sept. 13, 1963) , p. 7; Russell T. Hitt, "The New Pentecostalism," *Eternity*, July, 1963, reprint, p. 3.

4 "Divine or Devilish?" *Christian Herald*, May, 1964, pp. 14-16.

11:14 that Satan was busy even in Corinth: "For even Satan fashioneth himself into an angel of light" (ASV). Pentecostals themselves admit that sometimes the tongue-speaking which goes on in their churches may be a fanatical gibberish which is of the flesh rather than of the Spirit.[5] Whenever tongue-speaking ministers to personal pride, whenever it leads to emotional orgies in which all self-restraint is cast to the winds, whenever it causes bitter discord between Christians who ought to conduct themselves as one in Christ — surely the devil has had a hand in the situation![6]

Though I would grant that glossolalia may at times be demonically induced, I would be inclined to agree with Edman that this is not usually the case.[7] What about the second possibility, namely, that present-day tongue-speaking is a genuine gift of the Spirit? Once again, we cannot entirely rule out this possibility. We certainly cannot bind the Holy Spirit by suggesting that it would be impossible for Him to bestow the gift of tongues today! Who knows what the Spirit may still have in store for the church? Who knows what gifts of the Spirit may be given in the future to enable the church to meet specific new challenges?

We must, of course, grant that Paul does not forbid the use of glossolalia in I Corinthians 12 to 14. It must also be admitted that the gift of tongues had some value for Paul and for the church of that day; even Paul was led to thank God that he spoke with tongues more than all the Corinthians (chap. 14:18). Surely Paul would never have said this if glossolalia had no value whatever!

It is, however, a moot question whether the gift of

---

5 Brumback, *op. cit.,* p. 259.

6 Cf. K. Runia, "Speaking in Tongues Today," *Vox Reformata,* No. IV (May, 1965), pp. 42-44.

7 *Loc. cit.,* p. 15.

tongues, as a special gift of the Spirit, is still in the church today. In a previous chapter I have given some of the reasons why I believe we should have serious doubts about the continuance of glossolalia as a special gift of the Spirit; these reasons I do not intend to repeat here. If tongues as a gift of the Spirit should still be present in the church today, Pentecostals have no right to claim that the possession of this gift, even as an initial physical sign, proves that one has received the fullness of the Spirit. If the gift should still be present, the many restrictions with which Paul surrounds its use in I Corinthians 14 imply that glossolalia is not nearly as important as Pentecostals seem to think it is, and that it is by no means the *sine qua non* of spiritual maturity. And the baffling question remains: how can Pentecostals and Neo-Pentecostals be sure that what is going on in tongue-speaking circles today is the same thing that went on in New Testament days? Do we know exactly what the glossolalia practiced by the Corinthians was? If we do not know this, how can anyone be certain that what is taking place in tongue-speaking groups today is exactly the same as that which happened in the days of the New Testament church?[8]

I am inclined to agree with Donald S. Metz that glossolalia as we see it today is for the most part neither directly inspired by the Spirit nor directly induced by demons, but is a human reaction which has been psychologically induced.[9] This also appears to be the position of George B. Cutten, a recognized authority on tongue-speaking, who said, "As far as I know there is no case of speaking in strange tongues which has been strictly and scientifically

[8] It seems particularly difficult to maintain this identity when account is taken of the many centuries during which tongue-speaking was virtually absent from the church.

[9] *Speaking in Tongues*, p. 104. Dr. Metz is the head of the Department of Religion at Bethany Nazarene College.

investigated that cannot be explained by recognized psychological laws."[10] To the same effect is a statement by Psychiatrist Stuart Bergsma, Superintendent of Pine Rest Christian Hospital in Grand Rapids, Michigan. After mentioning a number of experiences which have helped him arrive at an evaluation of glossolalia, he says, "All these [experiences] have left me with the conviction that glossolalia especially can be psychologically explained and is not, in general, a 'spiritual' phenomenon."[11] Another Christian psychiatrist gives a similar evaluation, in an article in which he analyzes the phenomenon of tongue-speaking:

> The product of our analysis is the demonstration of the very natural mechanisms which produce glossolalia. As a psychological phenomenon, glossolalia is easy to produce and readily understandable.[12]

If the above analyses are correct, the question arises: what are the psychological mechanisms operative in glossolalia? When we reflect on the fact that glossolalia has appeared outside of the Christian religion in the past and still appears in other cultures today, it is not surprising that it has also cropped up in Christian circles.[13] Whatever motivated it in these other cultures could motivate

10 *Speaking With Tongues,* p. 181.

11 "Speaking With Tongues," Part II, *Torch and Trumpet,* XIV, 10 (Dec., 1964) , p. 10. (Note: These articles have been published under the same title in paperback by Baker Book House.)

12 E. Mansell Pattison, "Speaking in Tongues and About Tongues," *Christian Standard,* Feb. 15, 1964, p. 2. Dr. Pattison, a member of the Christian Association for Psychological Studies, is currently an instructor in psychiatry at the University of Washington School of Medicine.

13 "Tongues, Gift of," *Encyclopaedia Britannica,* 1964 ed., XXII, 288-89; P. Feine, "Speaking with Tongues," *Schaff-Herzog Encyclopaedia of Religious Knowledge* (Grand Rapids: Baker, 1960) , XI, 37-38; Donald Metz, *op. cit.,* pp. 24-27. See also above, p. 10, n. 2.

it among Christians. The emotional stimulation which often gives rise to tongues in non-Christian circles could also cause tongue-speaking among Christians.[14] It must be granted that tongue-speaking need not always occur in a situation which is highly charged emotionally, and that it may occur in a quiet, devotional atmosphere;[15] yet even in such circumstances strong emotional forces may be operative beneath the surface. One can certainly understand the appeal of the mysterious in an age which is predominantly rational. It may very well be that much tongue-speaking in non-Pentecostal groups today represents an emotional reaction against a coldly intellectual type of preaching or against a stereotyped, formalistic liturgy.

There are also other possibilities. L. M. Van Eetveld Vivier, in a doctoral dissertation on glossolalia, reports that a group of tongue-speaking Pentecostals whom he tested were found to have had "psychologically, a poor beginning in life characterized by insecurity, conflict, and tension."[16] Russell T. Hitt is of the opinion that many of those who have experienced the so-called "Spirit-baptism" have been suffering from deep personal or family problems, or are emotionally troubled about their own spiritual lives.[17] For such individuals tongue-speaking might provide a way of escape from pressing problems, or a way of gaining status otherwise denied them.

We can also well understand that the psychology of suggestion could play a large part in inducing glossolalia. When one belongs to a group in which it is expected that those most advanced spiritually will speak with tongues,

14 *Encyclopedia Britannica, loc. cit.,* p. 289.

15 Kelsey, *op. cit.,* p. 13.

16 Farrell, *loc. cit.,* p. 6. The dissertation, entitled simply *Glossolalia,* was written for the University of Witwatersrand, South Africa.

17 *Loc. cit.,* reprint, pp. 7-8.

when much emotional pressure is being applied in the pursuit of the gift of tongues, when seekers of the gift are even told to loosen the tongue by saying "ah-bah, ah-bah beta, beta," and the like,[18] it would be strange indeed if no one would begin to do what everyone was expecting.

Very helpful light is shed by Mansell Pattison on the psychological mechanisms which may be operative in glossolalia:

> Speech is a complex phenomenon involving both conscious, willful elements and unconscious, automatic patterns in psychological and physiological circuits. We are all aware of common distortions of normal speech. When excited we stutter, forget what we were saying, say something other than intended (slip of the tongue), or are rendered speechless! . . . Sometimes when starting to talk we get confused and tongue-twisted, saying a garble of sounds and syllables. People talking in their sleep often utter unintelligible jargon. So also do patients under sedation or anesthesia, or in partial coma.
>
> All of these examples indicate aberrations of our usual and normal speech patterns. We can observe that if our attention is diverted from our speech we may continue talking under the control of unconscious mechanisms which may or may not produce intelligible speech. Any of us could "speak in tongues" if we adopted a passive attitude about controlling our body and speech and had an emotional tension pressing for expression. A familiar example is the explosive, contagious laughter of a group which reaches a point where everyone is "too weak to move" from laughing. Trying to talk while thus laughing results in vocalizations which have all the characteristics of glossolalia.[19]

Dr. Pattison finds parallels to glossolalia in certain types of clinical situations:

18 Edman, *loc. cit.*, p. 16.
19 *Loc. cit.*, p. 2.

> . . . I can add my own observations from clinical experiences with neurological and psychiatric patients. In certain types of brain disorders resulting from strokes, brain tumors, etc., the patient is left with disruptions in his automatic, physical speech circuit patterns. If we study these "aphasic" patients we can observe the same decomposition of speech that occurs in glossolalia. Similar decomposition of speech occurs in schizophrenic thought and speech patterns, which is [*sic*] structurally the same as glossolalia.
>
> This data can be understood to demonstrate that the same stereotypes of speech will result whenever conscious, willful control of speech is interfered with, whether by injury to the brain, by psychosis, or by passive renunciation of willful control. This corroborates our previous assessment that glossolalia is a stereotyped pattern of unconsciously controlled vocal behavior which appears under specific emotional conditions.[20]

The conclusion at which Pattison arrives is that glossolalia may occur whenever conscious, willful control of speech is interfered with, and that in its present-day form it is usually a psychological accompaniment of intense or ecstatic emotional experiences.

But, one may say, if glossolalia today is for the most part not a gift of the Spirit but a phenomenon psychologically induced, how are we to account for the spiritual benefits people claim to have received from it? It should be observed first of all that tongues have not always brought a spiritual blessing, but that there are cases on record where

[20] *Ibid.* In this connection it is significant to note that at least two competent linguists, after analyzing taped samples of glossolalia, both came to identical conclusions: what they heard were not actual languages but types of ecstatic speech, with peculiar consonantal structure and very limited vowel sounds, which bore no resemblance to any language spoken on earth. See the letter to the editors by William E. Welmers, Professor of African Languages at the University of California in Los Angeles, in the Nov. 8, 1963, issue of *Christianity Today* (pp. 19-20) ; and the description of the analysis made by Dr. Eugene E. Nida of the American Bible Society in V. Raymond Edman's article, "Divine or Devilish," in the *Christian Herald* of May, 1964 (p. 16) .

what was passed off as the gift of tongues was later admitted to be a hoax, or where what was first thought to be of the Spirit was later ascribed to the flesh. We have already noted Warfield's reference to Robert Baxter of the Catholic Apostolic Church, who admitted that the tongues in which he and others had been speaking were by a lying spirit and not by the Spirit of the Lord. C. H. Darch, of Taunton, England, tells about a man who once claimed to have the gift of tongues, but who later told him, "I am now convinced, I had nothing of the kind."[21] D. Robert Lindberg, a graduate of Dallas Theological Seminary, who was a missionary in China for some years and is now a pastor in the Orthodox Presbyterian Church, tells how he once sought and experienced what was called the gift of tongues. Though at the time he felt something of the joy and thrill of which others had spoken, he was later constrained to re-evaluate this experience.[22] After making it very clear that he is not criticizing *persons* but a *movement,* and after having affirmed that he does not wish to deny that some have had a transforming experience through glossolalia, he goes on to say that he is now convinced that the tongue-speaking movement is not of God, but that it "has at its heart a false mysticism which is contrary to the word of God."[23] After giving seven reasons for this judgment, he concludes by asserting that the tongue-speaking we observe today is not of divine origin but is the result of "auto-suggestion, self-induced — piously, yes, but wrongly and unscripturally."[24]

I have in my files a personal letter from a man who was

---

[21] "The Gift of Tongues," *The Harvester,* XLIII, No. 8 (August, 1964) , p. 115.

[22] ". . . Try the Spirits . . .," *Presbyterian Guardian,* Vol. 34, No. 2 (Feb., 1965) , p. 19.

[23] *Ibid.,* p. 20.

[24] *Ibid.,* p. 22.

a Pentecostal pastor for nine years. During these years he spoke in tongues, considering his initial experience in tongue-speaking evidence of the baptism with the Holy Spirit. Later he became convinced that the particular emphases of the Pentecostal movement were not supported by Scripture; he left the Pentecostal church, and became a minister in another denomination. He is now certain that the tongue-speaking he did in the past was entirely of the flesh rather than of the Spirit. He writes:

> I do not believe tongues have any value as a devotional exercise, for I have proved this in my own life, for my devotion is more spiritual since I have refrained from speaking in tongues. My ministry has been more spiritual also and fruitful since I left the Pentecostal church, and I have no desire to ever return.

The man also states that he has never seen tongues legitimately used as a gift in the church during the years he was a Pentecostal minister. "There were times when people spoke in tongues in the church, but it never brought edification to the entire group."

As we noted earlier, however, many people claim that they have received genuine spiritual blessings through tongue-speaking, some even holding that the experience has transformed their lives. How are we to account for these claims? I believe we have the key to the solution of this problem in two statements made by two individuals to whom I have already referred. Dr. Pattison, at the end of his analysis of tongue-speaking, makes the following comment:

> Glossolalia has no intrinsic spiritual value. It may be the psychological accompaniment of a meaningful spiritual experience, but it must be seen as incidental in the attainment of spiritual goals.[25]

25 *Loc. cit.,* p. 2.

The significant words here are: "may be the psychological accompaniment of a meaningful spiritual experience." The other statement is from the former Pentecostal pastor's letter:

> In my evaluation of glossolalia in my own life, I would say it was entirely of the flesh in the final analysis. The many hours of honestly seeking the Lord, however, brought much blessing.

Here we see the same thought expressed, by one who himself spoke with tongues for nine years: though the glossolalia itself was not spiritually helpful, the seeking of the Lord which accompanied or preceded the glossolalia was. From the same letter I quote the following:

> The emphasis on prayer has brought a warmness of faith and Christian experience to the Pentecostal people, which is many times lacking in our churches. I feel most of the success in the charismatic movement today is because of a revolt against the dry rot of orthodox teaching which fails to appreciate the life of the Spirit.

Again, what is said here to be beneficial is not the tongue-speaking as such but the emphasis on prayer which goes with it.

I think we are ready now to see how a tongue-speaking experience can be a source of real spiritual blessing to people. When this is the case — and I do not deny that it may often be the case — I would suggest that what is really the source of the spiritual blessing is not the glossolalia as such but the state of mind of which it is said to be the evidence, or the spiritual disciplines which have preceded it. If a Christian has honestly sought to be more filled with the Spirit than he was before, and has yielded himself more completely to the Spirit's promptings, this is bound to bring spiritual rewards. If a Christian has been spending more time in prayer than he did before, earnestly seeking spiritual enrichment, this is bound to produce fruits. When, further, a person begins to speak with tongues in a small Neo-Pentecostal group, this phenomenon is the culmination of an experience of Christian fellowship, Bible study, and prayer in a small, closely-knit circle of spiritually minded friends — an experience which is bound to be profitable. In other words, we can account for the spiritual blessings experienced in these instances wholly apart from the tongue-speaking. I am not questioning the sincerity of the Christian brethren who have these experiences, nor the genuineness of their spiritual growth; I am only saying that it is very well possible that the key to these blessings was not the glossolalia itself but the seeking for a greater fullness of the Spirit which preceded it.

We return now to the question with which this chapter began: What is the challenge of Pentecostalism for the church today? Surely this new "outburst of tongues" has something to say to the rest of the church! The church may never be satisfied with itself; it must always continue to confess its spiritual poverty and its shortcomings. In movements like Pentecostalism and Neo-Pentecostalism we may hear the voice of God. If there were no shortcomings in the church, movements like this would never gain a foothold.

What, now, are some of the lessons the Pentecostal movement has been teaching the rest of the church? Let me briefly enumerate a few of these:

(1) The church today desperately needs a stronger emphasis on the need for being constantly filled with the Spirit of the living God. Apart from that Spirit all her busyness, all her organizations, all her machinery, will be powerless.

(2) The church must have a greater concern than before for satisfying man's emotional needs. Not that we need

to go to the extremes found in some Pentecostal churches where, it is to be feared, emotional excitement is sometimes mistaken for spirituality, and where the success of a service is sometimes judged by the pitch of emotional fervor which has been reached. Excessive emotionalism never glorifies God; "let all things be done decently and in order" (I Cor. 14:40). But man does have an emotional side, and the church must not neglect it. If we preach the unsearchable riches of Christ with the animation of a dead-tired radio announcer droning through a weather report, we shall probably succeed in driving people out of our churches. Those who leave one denomination to join another usually do not do so primarily for doctrinal reasons but because the church they are leaving fails to satisfy some of their basic needs. Unchurched people in the neighborhood will not be attracted by churches which are as cold as ice or by preachers who are as dry as dust.

(3) In the church we ought to leave more room for spontaneity in worship and more opportunity for audience response than we now do. I am not pleading for a liturgy of "holy disorder," but I am saying that a church service that is marked by what D. Andrew Blackwood at Princeton Seminary used to call "lameness, tameness, and sameness" will not be very helpful to people. Why should a single individual always be at the center of the liturgical service? Why should there not be more responses from the audience? If the current stress on the expert rendition of anthems by a few trained voices should involve a decreasing emphasis on spirited singing by the entire congregation, are we really making liturgical progress or are we slipping backwards?

(4) We can also learn anew from our Pentecostal and Neo-Pentecostal friends the importance of prayer and the fact of our constant dependence on God. Do we in our

strongly fortified ecclesiastical castles not sometimes substitute boards, committees, resolutions, and business meetings for prayer? Does not James still have a word for us, "Ye have not, because ye ask not"?

(5) We can learn anew the importance of being ready at all times to witness for our Lord, and the need for greater missionary zeal. Pentecostals are usually not afraid to witness, and their far-flung missionary endeavors put many other Christian groups to shame. As we saw before, it has been estimated that the band of Pentecostal missionaries on foreign fields some ten years ago was at least three and a half times as large as "normal" within the Protestant world.[26] Surely the Lord is speaking to the church today through this movement!

(6) From Neo-Pentecostals particularly we can learn anew the value of small-group meetings for Bible study, prayer, and Christian fellowship. In such meetings one is stimulated by the faith and testimony of others, and one is encouraged to enter into the lives of his fellow Christians in a way that is otherwise almost impossible in our large and scattered urban congregations. Small-group fellowships of this sort may provide one of the best ways in which the church of our time can meet the problem of increasingly de-personalized living.

Much more could be said about these things. We appreciate the warm evangelical spirit of our Pentecostal brothers. We appreciate their conservative theological position, and their opposition to theological liberalism.[27] We appreciate their tremendous evangelistic zeal, both at

[26] Nils Bloch-Hoell, *The Pentecostal Movement*, p. 90.

[27] It should, of course, be remembered that there are Pentecostal bodies, like the United Pentecostal Church, which are unitarian, denying that there are three Persons in the Trinity. Most Pentecostal groups, however, repudiate this teaching.

home and abroad, and their exemplary concern for reaching out with the gospel.

I should like at this point, however, to return particularly to the first point mentioned above, our need for being more filled with the Spirit of God. None of us would care to deny that this is the greatest need of the church today — the most important key to victorious Christian living and to a radiant Christian witness. Here is the real heartbeat of Pentecostalism. The emphasis on this Biblical truth by the modern tongue-speaking movement is its most significant contribution to the contemporary Christian world — a contribution for which we are deeply grateful.

To this indebtedness I want to do full justice. The church is often in danger of forgetting the importance of the ministry of the Spirit, and our day is no exception. All of us who teach or study theology should be ready to admit that the doctrine of the Person and work of the Holy Spirit has not been treated as thoroughly as has, for example, that of the Person and work of Jesus Christ. The most ambitious theological works on the Holy Spirit to date are still those of John Owen, the English Puritan, and Abraham Kuyper, the Dutch Calvinist, written in 1674 and 1888, respectively. We could well use a new treatment of this vital topic, which would take into account recent Biblical and theological developments. We are therefore grateful to both Pentecostals and Neo-Pentecostals for having revived the church's concern with the work and ministry of the Holy Spirit.

As has become evident, however, I do have serious difficulties with many Pentecostal teachings about the Spirit. I do not understand the Bible to teach that believers need to wait for a "baptism with the Spirit" before they can enjoy the fullness of the Holy Spirit. As a matter of fact, this teaching can be very misleading. Does it help or does it hinder to tell a Christian to wait for the Spirit to do something, when actually the next move, as far as tasting the fullness of the Spirit's power is concerned, is up to the believer himself?[28] May not the doctrine that one must "tarry" or "wait" for the Spirit-baptism, in fact, give believers a ready-made excuse for putting off full surrender to the Spirit for a long period of time? (think of the man who had been a "seeker" for ten years). Further, does it not introduce confusion into the entire issue when believers are taught that unless they have spoken with tongues, they lack the most important proof that they have received the fullness of the Spirit? Conversely, if the mere ability to speak with tongues is hailed as proof positive that one has received this fullness, will not such teaching rather tend to encourage a type of "post-Spirit-baptism" laxity? Is there not a very real danger that Christians who have received this alleged Spirit-baptism may now begin to think they have "arrived" spiritually, and therefore need no longer continue to "press on toward the goal"?

If it be true, however, as I have tried to show earlier, that the Holy Spirit is already dwelling within every regenerate and converted believer, then Pentecostalism and Neo-Pentecostalism are in error on this point. If after conversion the Spirit is already dwelling within, then we are not to wait for Him to descend upon us, but He is waiting for us to yield ourselves more fully to Him.

At this point the reader's attention is called to a very helpful little book from which I have profited greatly, *The Baptism and Fullness of the Holy Spirit,* by John R. W. Stott. This booklet contains the substance of an address

---

[28] It is not contended here that one can yield himself more fully to the Spirit in his own unaided strength. I am only saying that the Bible does not command believers to wait for a Spirit-baptism after conversion; it rather enjoins them to keep on walking in or by that same Spirit in whom they live (Gal. 5:25).

given at the Islington Clerical Conference on January 7, 1964.[29] While rejecting the position that every believer must experience a post-conversion Spirit-baptism attested by glossolalia, Dr. Stott agrees that many Christians need to be more filled with the Spirit than they are.

The point is: though Christians receive the Spirit at the time of conversion, they do not necessarily remain filled with the Spirit. They may drift away from doing the will of God and may become proud, quarrelsome, loveless, or self-indulgent. In such instances they will need once again to recover the fullness of the Spirit which they had when they were converted. It may very well be true of many of us today, in fact, that, though we have the Holy Spirit, the Holy Spirit does not have all of us. How, then, can we become more filled with the Spirit? The answer to this question is easy to state but hard to carry out: by yielding our lives more fully to the Spirit.

Consider, for example, the teaching of Ephesians 5:18-21:

> And be not drunken with wine, wherein is riot, but be filled with the Spirit; speaking one to another in psalms and hymns and spiritual songs, singing and making melody with your heart to the Lord; giving thanks always for all things in the name of our Lord Jesus Christ to God, even the Father; subjecting yourselves one to another in the fear of Christ (ASV).

This passage makes it very clear that the evidence of being filled with the Spirit is not a miraculous sign like glossolalia but consists of certain spiritual qualities and activities. How, according to this passage, does one reveal that he is filled with the Spirit? (1) By "speaking one to another[30]

---

29 Though originally published in England, the booklet can be obtained in the United States from the Inter-Varsity Press, 1519 North Astor, Chicago, Ill., 60610.

30 This translation is to be preferred to the KJ rendering, "speaking to yourselves." The Greek permits either.

in psalms and hymns and spiritual songs" — a probable reference to the activity of worshiping together; (2) by "singing and making melody with your heart[31] to the Lord" — the Spirit-filled believer will delight in singing God's praises from the heart; (3) by "giving thanks always for all things in the name of our Lord Jesus Christ to God, even the Father"; and (4) by "subjecting yourselves one to another in the fear of Christ" — the Spirit-filled Christian will not be marked by self-assertion but rather by self-submission. These, then, are the marks of a person who is filled with the Spirit.

As we return now to look at the command, "be filled with the Spirit," we notice three things about it:[32] (1) The verb is plural in number: "be all of you filled with the Spirit" (*plērousthe*). To be filled with the Spirit, therefore, is not a privilege reserved for the few; all believers are to be so filled. "The Holy Spirit's fullness, like sobriety and self-control, is obligatory, not optional."[33]

(2) The verb is in the passive voice: "be filled with the Spirit."[34] The thought is: let the Holy Spirit fill you. How can one do this? Obviously, by yielding wholly to the Spirit. The Spirit is not a substance which can be poured into one; He is a Person who dwells within believers, and we can be filled with Him only by yielding ourselves more and more to His blessed influence. Other Scripture passages shed light on how this yielding is to be carried out: "If we live in the Spirit, let us also walk in the Spirit"

---

[31] To be preferred to the KJ translation, "in your heart," which suggests that this praising is to be done silently. The Greek permits either translation.

[32] For these observations about the passage, I gratefully acknowledge my indebtedness to Mr. Stott (*op. cit.*, pp. 30-31).

[33] *Ibid.*, p. 31.

[34] Actually, the verb could be either a middle or a passive, but the passive sense seems to fit the meaning better here.

(Gal. 5:25); "as many as are led by the Spirit of God, they are the sons of God" (Rom. 8:14); "who walk not after the flesh but after the Spirit" (Rom. 8:4); "quench not the Spirit" (I Thess. 5:19); "grieve not the Holy Spirit of God, whereby ye are sealed unto the day of redemption" (Eph. 4:30).

(3) The verb is in the present tense in the Greek. Since the present tense in Greek signifies continuing action, the specific thrust of the present imperative is to indicate that something which has already begun is to continue, or that something which has not yet begun is to be done from now on as a continuing action.[35] The command, therefore, could well be translated: "keep on being filled with the Spirit," or "be continually filled with the Spirit." "The present imperative 'be filled with the Spirit' . . . indicates not some dramatic or decisive experience which will settle the issue for good, but a continuous appropriation."[36]

Notice that those addressed in this epistle are said to have been previously sealed in or by the Spirit (1:13, 4:30). In each of these two passages, the verb for *sealed* is in the aorist tense, which in Greek denotes a single, once-for-all action. As we saw earlier, we have no right to restrict this sealing of the Spirit to certain believers in distinction from others; every believer has been sealed by the Spirit, and has thereby been marked as one of God's own people. Comparing Ephesians 1:13 and 4:30 with 5:18, we learn that, though every believer has been sealed with the Spirit, every believer does not remain filled with the Spirit. Believers

35 F. Blass and A. Debrunner, *A Greek Grammar of the New Testament*, trans. R. W. Funk (Chicago: University of Chicago Press, 1961), sec. 336. Cf. A. T. Robertson, *Grammar of the Greek New Testament in the Light of Historical Research* (Nashville: Broadman Press, 1934), pp. 890, 950.

36 J. Stott, *op. cit.*, p. 31.

who have been sealed with the Spirit must be exhorted to be continually filled with the Spirit.

This is, of course, by no means an easy matter. The present imperative teaches us that one may never claim to have received this filling once and for all. Being continually filled with the Spirit is, in fact, the challenge of a lifetime. Nothing but continual prayer, continued faithful use of the means of grace, and constant watchfulness will enable a believer to keep on being filled with the Spirit.

There are other Scripture passages, however, which shed further light on this matter of continuing to be filled with the Spirit. Think, for example, of Paul's teaching in the fifth chapter of Galatians. The main thrust of the entire chapter is that God's people in New Testament times, in distinction from Old Testament believers, no longer need to be surrounded by a network of laws covering every possible moral, ceremonial, and spiritual contingency, but that they are now to walk by the Spirit who has been poured out upon the church. This is, in fact, the heart of Christian liberty as described in Galatians: to live by principle, under the guidance of the Holy Spirit, and in the light of God's Word. Now note what Paul says in 5:16, "This I say then, Walk in the Spirit, and ye shall not fulfil the lust of the flesh." The tense of the Greek word for *walk* is present, denoting continuing action: "keep on walking in the Spirit." This is not something we are to do occasionally, on certain days of the week, or when we are with certain types of people, but all the time. Life may not be divided into sacred and secular compartments; all of life is sacred.

> *Not for the lip of praise alone,*
> *Nor e'en the praising heart,*
> *I ask, but for a life made up*
> *Of praise in every part.*

One might ask, however, What does it mean to walk in or by the Spirit? I would suggest that it means two things: living by the Spirit's guidance, and living in the Spirit's strength. Living by the Spirit's guidance means waiting upon the Spirit, asking what the Spirit would have us do, where the Spirit would have us go. This includes daily study of the Scriptures, since the Spirit does not lead apart from the Word. Never may supposed direct revelations from the Spirit be hailed as superior to Scripture, nor may we simply wait for a kind of mystical "inner light." The better we know the Bible, the better we shall know how to walk by the Spirit. Negatively, walking by the Spirit means to silence the clamor of fleshly voices, to quell the energy of fleshly haste, to restrain every impulse till it has been proved to be of God. Positively, walking by the Spirit means to be guided by Him, to listen to Him moment by moment (as He reveals Himself in the Word), to yield to Him continually. As the compass needle turns toward the north, so our wills should regularly and habitually turn toward the Spirit.

Living by the Spirit's strength means leaning upon Him for the necessary spiritual power. It means *believing* that the Spirit can give us strength adequate for every need, *asking* for that power in prayer whenever we need it, and *using* that power by faith in daily life. The only way we can walk by the Spirit is to keep in constant touch with Him. The difference between a battery radio and a plug-in radio is that the latter must always be plugged in to the source of power in order to operate. God gives us strength, not on the battery principle, but on the plug-in principle; we need Him every hour.

When we keep walking by the Spirit, we may claim the promise: "and ye shall not fulfil the lust of the flesh." This is not a second command; it is a promise. God knows how easy it is even for a believer to slip into fleshly ways of living and thinking. But here is the promise: if we walk by the Spirit, we shall not fulfill fleshly lusts. For these two are opposite, like fire and water. It is impossible to fight sin by just saying no to it; the more one fights with a chimney sweep, the blacker one gets. We are not to be overcome by evil, but to overcome evil with good.

From Galatians 5:16, therefore, we learn again that being filled with the Spirit is far more than a momentary, instantaneous experience which a man may have on such and such a day, at 10:45 in the evening. It is rather a matter of a lifelong walk with God, involving a lifelong dependence on the Spirit's guidance and on the Spirit's strength.

Let us look at one more New Testament passage in this connection, Romans 12:1-2:

> I beseech you therefore, brethren, by the mercies of God, that ye present your bodies a living sacrifice, holy, acceptable unto God, which is your reasonable service.
> And be not conformed to this world: but be ye transformed by the renewing of your mind, that ye may prove what is that good, and acceptable, and perfect will of God.

In the earlier chapters of this epistle Paul has been setting forth in masterful fashion the way of salvation through faith in Christ. In the verses just quoted, which open the practical section of his letter, Paul sums up in one magnificent sentence the whole duty of the redeemed. "I beseech you," he says, "by the mercies of God" — those very mercies which he has so movingly and inspiringly described in earlier chapters — "that ye present your bodies a living sacrifice." The word *present,* customarily used to describe the bringing of a sacrifice to the temple priest, conjures up an image of a worshiper leading a sheep or a young bull to the temple court, in order to offer it as a sacrifice to God. Today, Paul is saying, you who are New Testament believers are still called upon to offer sacrifices to God. Only the sacrifices you must offer are no longer the bloody ones prescribed by Old Testament law — these have all been abolished. The sacrifices you must now bring are your own bodies. You must now offer your bodies to God as wholly, as irrevocably, as the Old Testament worshipers offered their rams or bullocks at the temple. Once you have given your bodies to God, you may never ask to have them back again. This offering is a once-for-all transaction; it is a decision which determines the course of a lifetime.[37]

Though this offering is to be presented once for all, however, it involves a continuing process of transformation. We learn this from verse 2. Here two imperatives are used, both in the present tense, the first in the form of a prohibition, the second in the form of a positive command. "Do not keep on being conformed to this world," Paul goes on to say, "but be continually transformed by the renewing of your mind." Do not keep on being patterned after this world — so much so that one would have to use a magnifying glass to tell the difference between you Christians and people of the world. Do not keep on trying to be as much like your worldly neighbors and acquaintances as possible, so that you will not stand out from the crowd or be thought narrow-minded or odd. But be continually transformed by the renewing of your mind. That is, let there be a glorious newness about you! Let there be new motives, new goals, new aims, new values, and new joys! Become growingly different from the world around you — the world of selfishness, greed, lust, and money-madness. For this tranformation is not something which

37 The tense of the verb for "present" is aorist, implying that this is a once-for-all type of action.

happens instantaneously; it is an ongoing process which takes a lifetime. Year by year, day by day, hour by hour, the transformation must go on. Only in the power of God can this take place. Only through persevering prayer can you continue to be transformed more and more into the image of Christ.

What do we learn, then, from Romans 12:1 and 2? We learn, first, that there must be a once-for-all yielding or presenting of our bodies to God as living sacrifices, so that His will may be done through us. This yielding should have taken place at the time of conversion. It may very well be, however, that a person who thinks he was converted at an early age finds that he never really yielded himself to God at that time, and therefore does so later in life. It would not be proper to call this a postconversion experience since the earlier experience was not a genuine conversion. Another possibility is far more common: Christians who have been truly converted may find themselves entering periods of spiritual laxity, so that they need from time to time to yield themselves anew to God. Such experiences, however, would be reconfirmations or reaffirmations of decisions which had been made before. One would not be justified in calling such reaffirmations "baptisms with the Spirit," since the Scriptures teach that the Spirit dwells within the believer from the moment of regeneration and conversion. The point of Romans 12:1, therefore, is that there must be a once-for-all yielding of ourselves to God, though this yielding may have to be reaffirmed from time to time.

This is, however, not the end of the matter. From the second verse of Romans 12 we learn that there must not only be a decisive yielding of our bodies to God, but that there must also be a continuing transformation of our lives, a daily renewing of our minds, an hourly proving of what is that good, acceptable, and perfect will of God. One simply cannot rest on his laurels after he has presented his body to God as a living sacrifice; he must continue to implement that yieldedness by daily sacrificial living. We see again, therefore, that yielding to God and being filled with His Spirit is not just a momentary, crisis type of experience, but is a spiritual discipline which involves a lifetime of consecrated, prayerful effort.

May we not at this point meet on common ground with our Pentecostal and Neo-Pentecostal friends? We praise God for whatever has been wrought by His Spirit in the hearts and lives of these our Christian brothers in the way of greater devotion to Christ, of warmer witness to His love, and of a closer walk with God. Will they not agree with us, however, that no matter what experiences one has had, no matter what "baptisms of the Spirit" he may believe he has received, no matter what spiritual gifts he may have exercised, he may never in this life count himself finally to have attained? Is not Spirit-filled living the challenge of a lifetime? And should we not all keep on saying what one Spirit-filled man, writing under the Spirit's inspiration, so eloquently said, "This one thing I do, forgetting those things which are behind, and reaching forth unto those things which are before, I press toward the mark for the prize of the high calling of God in Christ Jesus"?

Bibliography

BOOKS

WORKS BY PENTECOSTALS:

Brumback, Carl. *What Meaneth This?* A Pentecostal Answer to a Pentecostal Question. Springfield, Mo.: Gospel Publishing House, 1947.

Conn, Charles W. *Pillars of Pentecost.* Cleveland, Tenn.: Pathway Press, 1956.

Gee, Donald. *Concerning Spiritual Gifts.* Springfield, Mo.: Gospel Publishing House, [1947].

Nelson, P. C. *Bible Doctrines.* A Series of Studies Based on the Statement of Fundamental Truths . . . of the Assemblies of God. Rev. ed. Springfield, Mo.: Gospel Publishing House, 1948.

Riggs, Ralph M. *The Spirit Himself.* Springfield, Mo.: Gospel Publishing House, 1949.

Roberts, Oral. *The Baptism with the Holy Spirit and the Value of Speaking in Tongues Today.* 96 pp. Tulsa, Okla.: Oral Roberts, 1964.

Stiles, J. E. *The Gift of the Holy Spirit.* Burbank, Calif.: Mrs. J. E. Stiles, n.d.

Williams, Ernest S. *Systematic Theology.* 3 vols. Springfield, Mo.: Gospel Publishing House, 1953.

WORKS BY NON-PENTECOSTALS:

Anderson, Robert. *Spirit Manifestations and "The Gift of Tongues."* 31 pp. New York: Loizeaux Bros., n.d.

Bauman, Louis S. *The Tongues Movement.* 47 pp. Winona Lake: Brethren Missionary Herald Co., 1963.

Berkhof, Hendrikus. *The Doctrine of the Holy Spirit.* The Annie Kinkead Warfield Lectures, 1963-64. Richmond: John Knox Press, 1964.

Cutten, George Barton. *Speaking with Tongues*: Historically and Psychologically Considered. New Haven: Yale University Press, 1927.

Forge, James Norman. *The Doctrine of Miracles in the Apostolic Church*. Unpublished Master's Dissertation, Dallas Theological Seminary, 1951.

Hayes, D. A. *The Gift of Tongues*. New York: Eaton and Main, 1913.

Kelsey, Morton T. *Tongue Speaking*. An Experiment in Spiritual Experience. New York: Doubleday, 1964.

Kornet, A. G. *De Pinksterbeweging en de Bijbel*. Kampen: Kok, 1963.

Krajewski, Ekkehard. *Geistesgaben*. Eine Bibelarbeit über 1. Korinther 12-14. 64 pp. Kassel: J. G. Oncken, 1963.

Kuyper, Abraham. *The Work of the Holy Spirit*. Translated by Henri De Vries. Grand Rapids: Eerdmans, 1956 (copyrighted 1900; orig. Dutch ed., 1888-89).

Lombard, Emile. *De la Glossolalie chez les Premiers Chrétiens et des Phénomènes Similaires*. Lausanne: Bridel, 1910.

Mackie, Alexander. *The Gift of Tongues*. New York: George H. Doran, 1921.

Martin, Ira Jay, 3rd. *Glossolalia in the Apostolic Church*. A Survey Study of Tongue-Speech. Berea, Ky.: Berea College Press, 1960.

McConkey, James H. *The Three-Fold Secret of the Holy Spirit*. Pittsburgh: Silver Publishing Society, 1897.

Metz, Donald. *Speaking in Tongues: an Analysis*. Kansas City: Nazarene Publishing House, 1964.

Molenaar, D. *De Doop Met de Heilige Geest*. Kampen: Kok, 1963.

Mosiman, Eddison. *Das Zungenreden geschichtlich und psychologisch untersucht*. Tübingen: J. C. B. Mohr, 1911.

Owen, John. *On the Holy Spirit*. 2 vols. Philadelphia: Protestant Episcopal Book Society, 1862.

Sherrill, John L. *They Speak with Other Tongues*. New York: McGraw-Hill, 1964.

Stolee, H. J. *Speaking in Tongues*. Minneapolis: Augsburg Publishing House, 1963 (a reprint of *Pentecostalism,* copyrighted in 1936 by Augsburg Publishing House).

Stott, John R. W. *The Baptism and Fullness of the Holy Spirit*. 38 pp. Chicago: Inter-Varsity Press, 1964 (also published the same year by Inter-Varsity Fellowship in London, England).

Unger, Merrill F. *The Baptizing Work of the Holy Spirit*. Chicago: Scripture Press, 1953.

Vellenga, G. Y., and Kret, A. J. *Stromen van Kracht,* de Nieuwe Opwekkingsbeweging. 91 pp. Kampen: Kok, 1957.

Vivier, L. M. Van Eetveldt. *Glossolalia.* Unpublished M. D. Dissertation for the University of Witwatersrand, Johannesburg, South Africa, 1960.

Warfield, Benjamin B. *Miracles: Yesterday and Today.* True and False. Grand Rapids: Eerdmans, 1953 (originally published by Scribner's in 1918 under the title, *Counterfeit Miracles*).

Zodhiates, Spiros. *Speaking with Tongues,* and other titles. 6 booklets. Ridgefield, N. J.: American Mission to Greeks, 1964.

WORKS PRIMARILY HISTORICAL:

Bartleman, Frank. *How Pentecost Came to Los Angeles.* 2nd ed. Los Angeles: Frank Bartleman, 1925.

Bloch-Hoell, Nils. *The Pentecostal Movement:* Its Origin, Development, and Distinctive Character. Translated from the Norwegian by the author. London: Allen and Unwin, 1964.

Brumback, Carl. *Suddenly . . . From Heaven.* A History of the Assemblies of God. Springfield, Mo.: Gospel Publishing House, 1961.

Clark, Elmer T. *The Small Sects in America.* Rev. ed. New York: Abingdon, 1949.

Conn, Charles W. *Like a Mighty Army.* Cleveland, Tenn.: Church of God Publishing House, 1955.

Frodsham, Stanley H. *With Signs Following.* The Story of the Pentecostal Revival in the Twentieth Century. Rev. ed. Springfield, Mo.: Gospel Publishing House, 1946 (the first ed. of this book was published in 1926 by Gospel Publishing House).

Gee, Donald. *The Pentecostal Movement,* Including the Story of the War Years, 1940-47. London: Elim Publishing Co., 1949.

Hutten, Kurt. *Seher, Grübler, Enthusiasten.* 6th ed. Stuttgart: Quellverlag, 1960. Pp. 477-524 deal with the Pentecostal Movement.

Kendrick, Klaude. *The Promise Fulfilled:* A History of the Modern Pentecostal Movement. Springfield, Mo.: Gospel Publishing House, 1961.

Knox, R. A. *Enthusiasm.* A Chapter in the History of Religion, with Special Reference to the 17th and 18th Centuries. New York: Oxford University Press, 1950.

Lang, G. H. *The Earlier Years of the Modern Tongues Movement.* 79 pp. Wimborne, England: G. H. Lang, n.d.

Mead, Frank S. *Handbook of Denominations in the United States.* 2nd rev. ed. New York: Abingdon, 1961.

Steiner, Leonhard. *Mit folgende Zeichen.* Basel: Mission für das Volle Evangelium, 1954.

PERIODICALS

Bach, Marcus. "Whether There Be Tongues," *Christian Herald,* LXXXVII (May, 1964), 10-11, 20-22.

Beare, Frank W. "Speaking with Tongues: A Critical Survey of the New Testament Evidence," *Journal of Biblical Literature,* LXXXIII (Sept., 1964), 229-46.

Bergsma, Stuart. "Speaking with Tongues," *Torch and Trumpet,* XIV (Nov. and Dec., 1964), 8-11, 9-13.

Edman, V. Raymond. "Divine or Devilish?" *Christian Herald,* LXXXVII (May, 1964), pp. 14-17.

Ehrenstein, Herbert Henry. "Glossolalia: First Century and Today," *The King's Business,* Nov., 1964, pp. 31-34.

Farrell, Frank. "Outburst of Tongues: the New Penetration," *Christianity Today,* VII (Sept. 13, 1963), 3-7.

Finch, John G. "God-Inspired or Self-Induced?" *Christian Herald,* LXXXVII (May, 1964), 12-13, 17-19.

Hitt, Russel T. "The New Pentecostalism: An Appraisal," *Eternity,* XIV (July, 1963), 10-16.

Lapsley, James N., and Simpson, John H. "Speaking in Tongues," *Princeton Seminary Bulletin,* LVIII (Feb., 1965), 3-18.

Lindberg, D. Robert. ". . . Try the Spirits . . . ," *Presbyterian Guardian,* XXXIV (Feb., 1965), 19-24.

MacDonald, William G. "Glossolalia in the New Testament," *Bulletin of the Evangelical Theological Society,* VII (Spring, 1964), 59-68 (also available in pamphlet form from the Gospel Publishing House, Springfield, Mo.).

May, L. Carlyle. "A Survey of Glossolalia and Related Phenomena in Non-Christian Religions," *American Anthropologist,* LVIII (Feb., 1956), 75-96.

Pattison, E. Mansell. "Speaking in Tongues and about Tongues," *Christian Standard,* Cincinnati, Ohio, Feb. 15, 1964, pp. 1-2.

Phillips, McCandlish. "And There Appeared to Them Tongues of Fire," *Saturday Evening Post,* May 16, 1964, pp. 31-33, 39-40.

Runia, K. "Speaking in Tongues in the New Testament," "Speaking in Tongues Today," *Vox Reformata,* No. 4 (May, 1965), pp. 20-29, 38-46.

"Symposium on Speaking with Tongues," by J. H. Hanson, G. Krodel, H. Kaasa, and Oarne Suerala, *Dialog,* II (Spring, 1963), 152-59.

Trinity magazine, ed. Jean Stone. Published quarterly at P. O. Box 2422, Van Nuys, Calif. Various issues.

Van Elderen, Bastiaan. "Glossolalia in the New Testament," *Bulletin of the Evangelical Theological Society,* VII (Spring, 1964), 53-58.

View, ed. Jerry Jensen. Published quarterly at 836 S. Figueroa St., Los Angeles, Calif. Various issues.

Voice (Full Gospel Business Men's), ed. Jerry Jensen. Published monthly at 836 S. Figueroa St., Los Angeles, Calif. Various issues.

Index of Names and Subjects

Apostolic Overcoming Holy Church of God, 29

Assemblies of God, 26-27

Augustine, 16-17

Azusa Street Mission, 25-26

Baptism in, of, or with the Spirit, 35 (*see also* Spirit-baptism).

Baptists, tongue-speaking among, 32

Barratt, T. B., 26, 37

Baxter, Robert, 22

Bennett, Dennis, 31

Bertrand, Louis, 18

Biblical evaluation of tongue-speaking, 49-101; passages from the prophets, 50-53; passages showing that tongue-speaking was to remain in the church, 53-57; passages proving that tongue-speaking is evidence of Spirit-baptism, 57-81; tongue-speaking in I Corinthians 12-14, 81-101

Blessed Trinity Society, 32, 47

Bredesen, Harald, 32, 47

Campbell, Mary, 21

Catholic Apostolic Church, 21-22

Cevennes, the Little Prophets of, 19-21

Christenson, Larry, 32, 45

Christian Advance, 33

Chrysostom, 16

Church of God, 27-28

Church of God in Christ, 27

Corinthian Church, nature of, 85-86; attitude toward tongue-speaking found there, 85-86

Cornelius, 61, 71-73

Disciples at Ephesus, 73-77

Du Plessis, David J., 47

"Entire sanctification": defined, 35; relation to Spirit-baptism and tongue-speaking, 35-36

Episcopalians, tongue-speaking among, 31

Ewald, Tod, 46, 47

Ferrier, Vincent, 18

"Filled with the Spirit," 65-67; instances in Acts where people are said to be Spirit-filled but tongue-speaking is not mentioned, 79-80

Full Gospel Business Men's Fellowship, 33

Fundamental Truths, Statement of, 38

Gifts of the Spirit, 103-13; distinction between miraculous and ordinary gifts, 104-105; did the miraculous gifts remain in the church? 104-13

Glossolalia defined, 9, 10

History of tongue-speaking: from A.D. 100 to 1900, 10-24; the Pentecostal movement, 24-31; Neo-Pentecostalism, 31-33

Holy Spirit: His activity in regeneration and conversion contrasted with His activity in Spirit-baptism, 40-41; gifts of, 41, 103-13; need for being filled with, 114-15, 136, 139-49; proof of being filled with is not physical but spiritual, 116-17, 141-42; Christ must not be subordinated to, 117-19

Holy Spirit Fellowships, 33

International Church of the Foursquare Gospel, 28-29

Interpretation, gift of, 42

Irenaeus, 12-15

Irving, Edward, 21-22

Jansenists, 21

Latter-rain movement, 52-53

Lutherans, tongue-speaking among, 32

Methodists, tongue-speaking among, 32

Middle Ages, tongue-speaking during, 18-19

Montanism, 11-12

Neo-Pentecostalism, 31-33

Neo-Pentecostals: views of, on the relation between tongue-speaking and Spirit-baptism, 45-48; prefer to exercise glossolalia in private devotions or small groups, 48; tongue-speaking less emotionally charged among, 48; significance of tongue-speaking

for, 48; theological position of, 122-23

Ozman, Agnes, 24

Parham, Charles F., 24-25, 36

Paul: said to have begun to speak with tongues at time of conversion, 79; said to have favored gift of tongues, 85; did possess the gift, 92-93

Pentecost Day, events of, 67-69

Pentecostal Assemblies of the World, 30

Pentecostal churches: origin, 24-26; main bodies described, 26-30; geographical distribution of, 30; mission work of, 30; number of adherents, 30-31

Pentecostal Church of God in America, 29

Pentecostal Holiness Church, 29-30

Pentecostal movement, 24-31

Pentecostalism: lessons we can learn from, 136-39; its most important contribution, 139

Presbyterians, tongue-speaking among, 31-32

Prophecy, superior to tongue-speaking, 89-96, 98-99

Reformed, tongue-speaking among, 32

Reformers on tongue-speaking, 19

Roberts, Oral, 29

Samaritans, 69-71

"Sealed with the Spirit," 63-65

Seymour, W. J., 25-26

Significance of tongue-speaking for Pentecostals, 35-48

Spirit-baptism: defined, 35; relation to sanctification, 35-36, 119: a "second work of grace" after regeneration, 36; relation to tongue-speaking, 24-26, 36-37,

38, 39, 40, 45-48; should be sought by all, 38-39; blessings resulting from, 38-39; relation to the new birth, 38-39; importance of, 39-40; description of, 40; relation to conversion, 40-41, 119; conditions for obtaining, 58-59; Biblical treatment of, 59-63; summary of Biblical teaching on, 81; the need for after conversion not taught in Scripture, 113-16; Pentecostal teaching on tends to create two levels of Christians, 119-20; doctrine of not discovered until the twentieth century, 121; Pentecostal teaching on misleading and erroneous, 139-40

Stone, Jean, 47

"Tarrying meetings," 59, 78-79
Tertullian, 15-16
Theological evaluation of tongue-speaking, 103-23
Theology of Pentecostalism: discussion of, 35-48; evaluation of, 103-23; teaches that a spiritual blessing must be attested by a physical phenomenon, 116-17; implies a kind of subordination of Christ to the Holy Spirit, 117-19; tends to create two levels of Christians, 119-20; implies that the church has been without a leader from the end of the first century to the beginning of the twentieth, 120-22
"Third Force in Christendom," 30
Tongues, devotional use of, 42; teaching of I Corinthians on, 98-101
Tongues, gift of: distinguished from tongues as evidence of Spirit-baptism, 38-39, 41; two-fold operation: devotional and congregational, 42; must be in-

terpreted when used in a church service, 42; value of, 84-85
Tongue-speaking: defined, 9; found in non-Christian religions, 10, 129; occurred only occasionally from 100 to 1900, among minority groups, 23, 112-13; reasons for this disappearance, 23-24; initial sign of Spirit-baptism, 38-39, 45-48; distinction between tongue-speaking as evidence of Spirit-baptism and as gift, 38-39, 41, 84; importance of, 39-40; described, 42-44; relative infrequency in the book of Acts, 79-81; relative infrequency in the New Testament, 111-12; spiritual blessings associated with, 125-26; demonically instigated? 126-27; a genuine gift of the Spirit? 127-28; a human reaction psychologically induced? 128-32; psychological mechanisms operative in, 129-32; instances where it was said to be of the flesh, 132-34; how to account for spiritual blessings received from, 135-36
Tongue-speaking in I Corinthians: differences between it and the tongue-speaking recorded in Acts, 82-83; does not prove that tongue-speaking is evidence of Spirit-baptism, 84, 96-97; inferior to prophecy, 89-96; teaching of I Corinthians 12-14 on summarized, 96; limited value ascribed to by Paul, 110-11
Tongue-speaking, still in the church today? 103-13
Trinity magazine, 32

United Pentecostal Church, 28

Xavier, Francis, 18

Index of Scriptures

ISAIAH

28:11, 12   50-51

JOEL

2:23   51-53

MATTHEW

3:11   59
7:22-23   117

MARK

1:8   59
16:17-18   53-56, 106

LUKE

3:16   59
16:31   110
24:49   78-79

JOHN

1:33   59
16:14   118

ACTS

1:5   60
2:4ff.   67
2:33   60
2:38   68-69
4:31   65-66
8:4-24   69-71
10:44-46   71-73
10:46   61
11:15-17   72-73

11:16   60, 81
14:3   107
19:1-7   73-77

ROMANS

8:9   114
12:1, 2   146-49
12:6-8   86
15:15-19   108

I CORINTHIANS

3:16   114
12-14   110-11, 127
12:8-10   86, 93, 103, 104
2:12-27   86-87
12:13   61-63
12:28   56-57, 86, 103, 106
12:30   87
12:31   88
13:1-3   88-89
13:8   106-107
14:1   89
14:3, 4   89, 99
14:5   90, 93, 99
14:6-13   90-91
14:14, 15   91, 92, 99-100
14:14-19   91-93
14:18   79, 92, 127
14:20-25   93-94
14:21   51

14:24-25   111
14:26-33   94-95
14:39   95-96, 99
14:40   137

II CORINTHIANS

12:12   107-108

GALATIANS

3:28   120
5:16   144-46
5:22-23   116
5:25   114, 142-43

EPHESIANS

1:13   63-65, 66, 115, 143
4:11-12   86, 104
4:30   64-65, 143
5:18   66-67, 115
5:18-21   141-44

I TIMOTHY

3:1-13   112

TITUS

1:5-9   112

HEBREWS

2:3-4   108-109

JAMES

5:7, 8   52-53